Going to Univ

More and more students in the world now decide to undertake their university studies in another country to their own. They see advantages of quality, value and experience in studying abroad and rightly see the experience as preparation for life and a big plus for their CVs in an increasingly interconnected world and job market. The world language is now undisputedly English and even universities in non-English speaking countries such as Holland and Denmark, universities that want to attract international students, are switching to teaching university programmes in English. This makes for an unparalleled opportunity for UK students, particularly at a time when UK university fees are increasing significantly.

This guide gives an overview of the opportunities available to UK students across the world, from the English speaking countries of the USA, Canada, Australia and New Zealand, to Asia (India, Hong Kong, Malaysia and Singapore), to offers nearer home, in Europe. As well as giving information on what is available, this book also explains:

- the education systems and academic cultures;
- the academic demands of the different destination countries;
- application procedures;
- information on living (accommodation, food and entertainment).

There are self-development exercises to help with the process of cultural readjustment that a UK student is likely to undergo and needs to understand.

Going to University Abroad covers information for both undergraduate and post-graduate programmes and recommends ideal destination countries for these. It is essential reading for students planning to study abroad.

Martin Hyde is an expert in international university education. He has extensive experience of working in education, initially in Morocco and the Dominican Republic, and then as a UK university lecturer involved with educational projects across the world. His experience also involves having worked as Assistant Director in a UK international office and being responsible for UK student study abroad placements. He has also recently written a guide to UK university life for international students.

Anthony Hyde is a recent graduate of the University of Oxford in Philosophy and Modern Languages. As part of his degree he studied and worked in both Spain and Argentina. He is currently working in Higher Education, and has undertaken extensive research into study abroad markets for UK students.

Going to University Abroad

A guide to studying outside the UK

Martin Hyde
with Anthony Hyde

Routledge
Taylor & Francis Group

LONDON AND NEW YORK

First published 2014
by Routledge
2 Park Square, Milton Park, Abingdon, Oxon OX14 4RN

and by Routledge
711 Third Avenue, New York, NY 10017

Routledge is an imprint of the Taylor & Francis Group, an informa business

British Library Cataloguing in Publication Data
A catalogue record for this book is available from the British Library

Library of Congress Cataloging in Publication Data
Hyde, Martin, 1960–
    Going to university abroad : a guide to studying outside the UK / Martin
    Hyde with Anthony Hyde.
        pages cm.
    1. Foreign study. 2. British students–Foreign countries. I. Hyde, Anthony,
    1990- II. Title.
    LB2376.6.G7H925 2014
    370.116–dc23   2013026409

ISBN: 978-0-415-53799-5 (hbk)
ISBN: 978-0-415-53800-8 (pbk)
ISBN: 978-1-315-85026-9 (ebk)

Typeset in Galliard
by Keystroke, Station Road, Codsall, Wolverhampton

MIX
Paper from
responsible sources
FSC   FSC® C013056
www.fsc.org

Printed and bound in Great Britain by
TJ International Ltd, Padstow, Cornwall

Contents

Chapter 1

Introduction to the guide

This chapter will first introduce you to the concept of studying abroad and the various issues that need to be considered when embarking on undertaking this life-changing move. It begins by explaining the historical growth of international universities in the world and the growing opportunities that are becoming available for UK students as a result of this. It also covers some of the key considerations that need to be taken into account for anyone wishing to embark on study abroad. In Chapter 2, the issues of understanding differences in educational approaches and understanding how to adapt linguistically, educationally and culturally are focussed upon. The remaining chapters then explain in detail the study abroad opportunities open to UK students offered by various world destinations. The countries focussed upon are first those of the English speaking world: the USA, Canada, Australia, New Zealand, South Africa and Ireland and then four other major potential destinations are presented in depth: Europe, Hong Kong, China and Singapore. Following these are chapters on emerging destinations for study abroad. These look at some of the less well-known countries that are currently opening up as international options for study abroad. The guide is aimed at UK undergraduate and postgraduate students alike and focusses on study abroad opportunities conducted in the medium of the English language.

The historical perspective: origins and spread of the modern university

The origin of the word 'university' is from the Latin 'universitas'. It described the special associations of teachers and students in medieval European towns who were awarded collective rights by the ruling town councils, princes or religious institutions. One key right was the right to grant a degree.

A key notion for the founding of these institutions was that of 'academic freedom' – i.e. the idea that students and faculty members should be able to pursue enquiry free from persecution. The first institution to develop such a noble principle was the University of Bologna (Italy) – which is Europe's oldest university.

To celebrate the 900th anniversary of the founding of this university (1088) and the protection of this ideal, a 'Magna Charta Universitatum' was signed on

18 September 1988 by 430 international university rectors. Each year more universities worldwide add their signatures to the charter.

In the UK, it is generally agreed Oxford has a claim to have originated as an institution of higher learning in 1096. It was not officially awarded a charter by Papal Bull until 1254 however.

Institutions of higher learning can also be found to have existed in the ancient cultures of Greece and India, the latter possibly laying claims to some of the oldest, with, for example, the University of Takshashila which was established in North West India around 700 BC.

There is also an argument that the origins of the concept of the university can be traced to the Islamic world. Al-Azhar in Cairo was founded in 969 AD and the Qarawiyyin Mosque in Fez (Morocco) was founded around the same time. However, their founding was primarily for Islamic religious instruction and study which is different from the objectives of the European university. In sum, the origin of the modern concept of a degree awarding university (one that awards Bachelor's, Licentiate and Master's degrees and Doctorates) is generally considered to be of European origin.

The advance of university education across the world

The concept of the European university was spread around the world as a result of European colonialism: by the British in Asia and Africa and the Spanish in Central and South America. Countries that were once under colonial rule, once gaining independence from their colonial powers, have been keen to develop and expand their higher education sector.

Medieval European universities structured 'knowledge' in various ways and this accounts for the development of a faculty structure. Indeed universities today still very much follow the pattern of seeing knowledge as located in faculties, such as, for example, the faculties of Philosophy, Letters, Law and Medicine. Within these faculties specific subjects of study (disciplines) were then grouped.

This concept of the university, and the value of knowledge in these disciplines, spread from the early modern period onwards across the globe, replacing other systems of higher learning. The spread can be seen to have developed in the following manner:

Period	World region
Eleventh–twelfth centuries	Western Europe
Fourteenth–fifteenth centuries	Eastern Europe
Sixteenth century	Americas
Nineteenth century	Australasia
Nineteenth–twentieth centuries	Asia and Africa

Early student mobility

Within universities in Europe, as they developed, differences in subject matter specialisms began to separate the north from the south. Italian universities tended to focus on law and medicine, whereas Northern European universities focussed on the arts and theology. Because there also developed differences in the quality of teaching in these areas, even since medieval times, scholars were already travelling north or south, based on their interests and their means.

The spread of universities was rapid: by the end of the eighteenth century there were 143 universities in Europe, with the highest concentrations in the German Empire (34), Italian countries (26), France (25) and Spain (23).

The most recent world list of universities undertaken in 1997 noted there were now 8,861 universities in 203 counties in the world, making a formidable choice for international students to choose from! Universities in the world are increasingly linking up with each other – one organisation, the International Association of Universities has over 600 members (see www.iau-aiu.net/).

Quality and institutional accreditation

Although world universities co-operate with each other, universities are also in competition with each other. Nation states increasingly look to their university sector to compete with other nations in the 'knowledge economy'. This means competing to secure the top professors and high achieving students (especially at research level) and to encourage them to locate in their countries, thus providing spin-off economic benefits. This competition has spawned many worldwide league tables which are used to compare the world's universities in terms of their standards and prestige.

University world ranking systems

- The Academic Ranking of World Universities (ARWU): www.arwu. org/
- QS World University Rankings: www.topuniversities.com/university-rankings
- Times Higher Education World University Rankings: www.timeshigher education.co.uk/world-university-rankings/

University world rankings are sites designed to try to help international students make a choice from the vast array of offers. It is wise, however, to consider that national papers may well have more information on universities within their own countries (local knowledge) and also that caution is best practised when checking these lists, as sometimes their objectivity may be felt to be coloured by national or political ideology!

Another way that a student can check on the quality of an institution is to look at its accreditation.

International business school accreditation

Besides there being national accreditation bodies set up in countries by national Ministries of Education (MoEs), to oversee their country's education standards, there have also developed international (privately run) accreditation bodies. These perform a supra-national accreditation function similar to national-level MoEs. They are often subscribed to by private universities and institutions that fall outside, or do not wish to be governed by, a national MoE. International accreditation is a process that many international business schools volunteer for in order to reassure applicants that the school in question offers programmes that have achieved a certain quality standard.

As there are over 12,400 business school institutions worldwide, having accreditations is one way that students can differentiate between them when making a choice over which one to attend.

In fact there are three principal international accreditation bodies used by business schools. These are shown in Table 1.1. Table 1.2 gives the other recently developed bodies.

Note: The Council for Higher Education Accreditation (www.chea.org/) is the non-governmental body that acts as the quality assurance agency for US Higher Education (the USA does not have government controlled regulation) and this organisation also maintains a database of accreditation bodies that have been allowed CHEA membership. This is a useful website to check out accreditation bodies used by private universities and business schools.

Table 1.1 Three principal international accreditation bodies

Name of body	Acronym and website	Further information
The Association to Advance Collegiate Schools of Business	AACSB www.aacsb.edu/	Started in Canada in 1916 but now international in scope. It is the oldest and most recognised body with more than 1,100 members.
European Quality Improvement System (EFMD)	EQUIS www.efmd.org/ accreditation-main/equis	Created in 1997, it is of European origin but now international. There are over 120 members in over 30 countries.
The Association of MBAs	AMBA www.ambaguide.com/	Established in 1967, it is UK-based. Over 150 business schools in around 70 countries are members.

Table 1.2 Other recently developed bodies

Name of body	Acronym and website	Further information
The International Assembly of Collegiate Business Education	IACBE http://iacbe.org/	Founded in 1997. It was recognised in 2011 by the Council for Higher Education Accreditation (CHEA) in the USA. It has accredited 200 institutions worldwide.
The Central and East European Management Development Association International Quality Association	CEEMAN IQA www.ceeman.org/	Established in 1993 it began offering International Quality Accreditation (IQA) from 1998. It mainly operates on a regional level in Central and Eastern Europe and has 210 members from over 50 countries.

Professional accreditation

Each profession also has its own international and national accreditation bodies: Medicine, Dentistry and Veterinary Medicine are examples of this. The important thing is ensuring that the programme you study abroad is recognised for the purposes of eligibility to register by the professional regulatory bodies for that profession in the UK or in the destination country you want to practice in after graduating. For Medicine this is the General Medical Council (GMC) (www.gmc-uk.org/); for Dentistry it is the British Dental Association (www.bda.org/); for Veterinary Medicine it is the Royal College of Veterinary Surgeons (RCVS) (www.rcvs.org.uk/) and for nursing it is the Nursing and Midwifery Council (NMC) (www.nmc-uk.org/). If overseas medical universities also offer validation by international bodies, such as the US Educational Commission for Foreign Medical Graduates (ECFMG), this is a possible advantage as it widens the pool of international locations where a graduate in medicine can apply to be registered for practice. Most countries, however, have their own procedures for international medicine graduates (IMGs) to follow in order to be able to register to practice. In the USA, this is the above mentioned ECFMG. This body controls those who can take, and uses the results of, a three-stage examination system called the United States Medical Licensing Examination (USMLE); in Australia to be licensed to practice, IMGs must obtain certification from the Australian Medical Council (AMC) and in Canada IMGs must pass a Licenciate of the Medical Council of Canada (LMCC) evaluating examination. It is similar within all the medical professions: e.g. veterinary colleges may offer accreditation by the American Veterinary Medical Association (AVMA) or the European Association of Establishments for Veterinary Education (EAEVE).

As a general rule of thumb, university provision in many countries can be divided into two distinct sectors – although the boundary between the two is becoming blurred over time: the traditional older research-focussed university sector and the more vocationally oriented university sector. The UK bears witness to this division with the Russell Group of universities and the 1992 group of universities which developed from the former polytechnics. Countries usually have a system of vocational training colleges where young people learn the practical skills of trades, which in the UK tends to be the main remit of the Colleges of Further Education (FE Colleges). It is important to distinguish between these types of higher education providers to make sure you apply for the type of programme you wish to undertake.

Current student mobility

Nowadays it is estimated there are about 3.6 million students studying at a university outside their own country (international students). This is a trend that has been increasing year on year by 12 per cent and is likely to increase significantly over the next decade. The main destination countries have been and continue to be the main English speaking countries of the USA, UK, Canada and Australia, as well as EU countries such as Germany and France. However, as universities in non-English speaking countries develop their English medium programmes, these countries are beginning to compete with the former countries for the growing pool of international students. Tables 1.3 and 1.4 show the current top destination

Table 1.3 Regions that host the largest number of internationally mobile students

Region	Number of internationally mobile students (%)
North America and Western Europe	58
East Asia and the Pacific	21
Central and Eastern Europe	9

Table 1.4 UK student mobility

Country	Number of students
USA	8,783
France	2,704
Ireland	1,804
Australia	1,661
Germany	1,342
Canada	807
Spain	531
New Zealand	505
Japan	479
Czech Republic	412
Norway	338
Switzerland	336
Brazil	331
Austria	318
Netherlands	232

regions of the world for international students (anyone studying for a higher degree outside their own country) and the destinations of English students in the world.

In 2011–12 there were some 23,000 UK students studying abroad (statistics taken from UNESCO Institute for Statistics, www.uis.unesco.org). This is less than half of the number from similar sized countries such as France and Germany. The chart shows that the USA is the top destination for UK students currently. It is worth noting that such data is very hard to obtain and present accurately and that in fact national statistics, by country, may give differing results. However, it does provide a rough overview.

The financial picture

In order to obtain a quick overview of the financial difference in terms of tuition fees (light grey) and living costs (dark grey) from various study destinations around the world, the following chart offers a rough guide:

Table 1.5 Overall average cost of tuition and living (per year) by country destination for international study abroad students

Destination		
USA	£18k	£12k
Canada	£12k	£10k
Australia	£16k	£12k
New Zealand	£12k	£10k
South Africa	£3k	£5k
Ireland	£10k	
EU Denmark	£12k	
EU Holland	£2k	£10k
E Europe	£8k	£4k
China	£3k	£4k
Hong Kong	£10k	£12k
Singapore	£14k	£6k
Malaysia	£4k	£4k
India	£6k	£4k
Compared to		
England	£9k	£8k
Wales	£3k	£8k
Scotland	£7k	

The following is a useful website for comparing the cost of living in various international locations: http://www.numbeo.com/

Here you are able to check out the cost of living in each country and also refine this to specific locations in each country. There is often a surprising difference between cities within countries and this may influence your choice.

The fact that tuition fees in the UK have risen to up to £9,000 per year may well be a catalyst for more UK students to consider studying abroad, despite the fact that student loans from the Student Loans Company (SLC) are available to UK students for study in the UK as well as university bursaries and grants for students from families with low income. While repayment terms are not high (currently 9 per cent on any income above the £21,000 salary threshold), the idea of 30 years of debt repayments, on top of other life expenses (mortgages, car loans, etc.), may be off-putting.

One of the drawbacks to studying abroad is that maintenance loans, available for living costs if you study in a UK university, are not available if you study abroad (EU included), and SLC tuition fee loans are not available to UK students for studying abroad either. Overall, however, if living costs each year in the UK are some £8,000 and tuition fees are £9,000 per year, the total cost of studying at a university for a three-year Bachelor's degree (if you do not live at home) is about £50,000.

The fact is that currently to study for the same degree in an EU country, where tuition is either free or much less expensive, is likely to cost about half this amount (calculated at £8,000–£9,000 per year on living costs).

On the other hand, to study abroad in the USA or Australia, UK students (unless they are in receipt of scholarships) need to pay the full overseas student fees, and only at the lower end are these at a similar level to UK home student tuition fee rates. The total cost of studying a degree in the USA (which is four years in duration) can easily be two to three times the cost of studying for a degree in the UK.

Before undertaking study abroad it is useful to research your financial options and undertake a realistic assessment of your financial possibilities. To this end the following questions may be of use:

1   Are you able to draw down any maintenance loans in the country you are going to study in? If so how do you obtain these?
2   Are you able to find any loans available in the UK for studying abroad? Can you secure any scholarships?
3   How much is it realistically going to cost you to live each year abroad in the country you have chosen? Note that the cost of living can vary a great deal

from country to country and region to region. Are you going to a more expensive country to live in or a cheaper one than the UK? Are your needs lavish or can you live modestly?

4   What is the current exchange rate between the Pound Sterling and the currency of the country you are going to study in? Is this likely to change favourably or unfavourably for the Pound Sterling over the medium term?

5   What are the possibilities of getting part-time work as an international EU student? How well is this remunerated?

But money and finance are not the only drivers of UK student interest in studying abroad. In fact the three top motivators according to recent research (BIS: Department for Innovation & Skills, Research Paper No. 8, 'Motivations and Experiences of UK Students Studying Abroad', January 2010, University of Dundee, URN 10/527. www.bis.gov.uk), found them to be: 1) the possibility of attending a world class university; 2) adventure; and 3) seeing the move as the first step to an international career.

International university English medium programme provision

The spread of the English language as the international language of academia appears to be growing and is not only the case in the private, but also in the public university sector. One reason for this is that the majority of high impact academic journals now publish in English. Even though there is a growing challenge to the dominance of English in research publications from countries such as China, the English language is now the *de facto* language of international research publications and so it is essential to be able to operate in English to be up to date in a field.

Another factor is that many universities in Western Europe, East Asia or the Middle East are now international in the sense that not only their student body, but their teaching faculty, is increasingly drawn from countries from all over the world. These 'international universities' increasingly teach programmes in English to cater for this mix of international students and teachers.

All of this means that for the native English speaking student a wealth of study opportunities for university programmes across the world has opened up, and not just in the traditional English speaking countries of the UK, USA and Australasia. The choice is expanding year on year.

The recognition of UK educational qualifications for study abroad

Generally UK educational certificates such as GCSEs and A Levels are respected as *bone fide* qualifications for study in universities everywhere abroad. Many universities in the world use various international databases to match UK qualifications to the local equivalents and there are often lists of equivalencies posted on MoE or university websites by overseas universities that you can consult.

One of the problems of matching qualifications, however, is the wide discrepancy between different national grading systems and UK grade equivalencies. The UK system of A–E grades at GCSE and A Level does not translate easily into grade point averages (GPAs). Overseas universities that have experience of applicants from the UK will probably have worked out a system for calculating the equivalencies themselves; inexperienced ones may well not have done. The same applies for those wanting to apply for a Master's programme, and translating the UK system of awarding a 1st, 2:1, 2:2 or 3rd into GPAs. The stipulated entry grades may vary from university to university and from programme to programme and, at times, may be based on a less than perfect understanding of the UK grading system. It is important to contact the overseas university's website or their international students' admissions office to check what the target grades for entry for the programme you wish to study are. It is also a good idea to accompany any application with a brief description of the grading system used for your certificates to help the overseas university decision makers (who may well be the academic programme directors of the programme you wish to study) understand exactly what the grades you have mean in real terms, i.e. let them know if they serve for studying a similar programme in a UK university, for example.

Legalisation of certificates

Unlike in the UK, when you apply to overseas universities, you may well need to legalise the copies of certificates you send off to the university with your application form. This is a safeguard for the overseas university to ensure the certificates you have are valid and not fraudulent. The UK may generally be quite free from certificate fraud, and UK students do not generally use the search for a student visa as an excuse to enter a country to work there illegally, but there are many countries in the world where fraud and visa abuse is a big issue, and overseas universities find they need to apply strict regulatory processes to avoid falling victim to this, and these rules generally apply to all overseas students, so as not to discriminate.

This means there is often an extra cost to an overseas university application, besides other costs such as application fees: this is the cost of legalisation of certificates. Most countries in the world to which you are likely to apply to study in a university will be signatories to The Hague Convention, which means that you only have to have your certificates legalised by a Notary Public in the UK and then have each certificate, once thus legalised, issued with an Apostille Certificate by the Foreign Office. The fees for the Notary Public and the Apostille Certificate can vary depending on the Notary Public's rates and the quantity of documents that need legalising for your application. You should, however, be prepared to spend several hundred pounds on this process.

Education agencies

All of this may appear quite taxing and difficult to undertake by oneself and it is understandable that many students decide to use the services of an education agency to help them undertake an application.

There are various types of agency available – some specialising in country specific or programme specific information. Others offer application procedure advice and help at a more general level. It is worth checking what fees education agencies charge for their services and it is also worth checking admission fees and procedures at the original university websites that you are interested in applying to. This is to ensure that you are not paying over the odds for the service offered. Some other education agencies, such as Outreach Education (www.outreacheducation.co.uk), offer free information and application management services.

Staying safe and staying healthy

It is sensible before setting off to a foreign destination as an international student to check with the Foreign and Commonwealth office (FCO) about your destination. The FCO gives up to date advice on the political and social situations in countries.

> The following website gives up to date information on foreign destinations: www.gov.uk/foreign-travel-advice

You also need to update yourself on the health situation in the country you are planning to study in and ensure that you are up to date on the recommended vaccinations. You can check the 'Travel Health' section of the NHS website (www.nhs.uk/travelhealth) for up to date information regarding this.

It is also wise and at times obligatory to take out travel and health insurance, at least for an initial period, until, if this exists, and is robust enough, you take out a university recommended policy for local health cover. There are many companies offering this service so it is good to shop around.

> The following site offers good advice on staying healthy abroad: www.british council.org/higher-education/uk-students-abroad/health

Chapter 2

Adapting to the new cultural environment

This chapter will focus upon you as a cultural being and try to explain the challenges and necessary self-knowledge and strategies you will need to be able to fully benefit from and succeed as a student studying abroad. From the diagram below you can see that when you choose to live and study abroad you can be pictured as if at the centre of an onion, with different layers of culture surrounding you. The first layer is the new classroom and the academic culture you are in, the second is the new university with its different administration and general procedures, the third layer is the social life associated with the university environment (campus or student life), the fourth layer is the specific town or region you are in and the immediate life outside the university and the fifth layer is the new

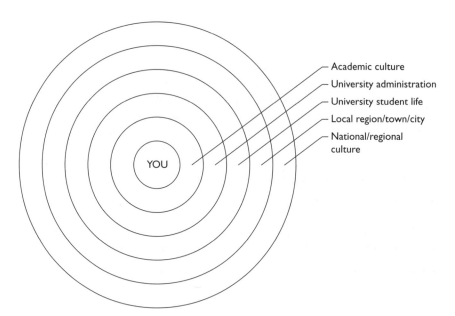

Figure 2.1 You and the cultural influences upon you as an international student.

national/regional culture (political, historical, social) that you are now immersed in. In reality these layers intermesh to produce the new environment you will be studying and living in and that you have to make sense of.

One of the key challenges, particularly early on when participating in a study abroad programme, is that of adapting to the new educational, linguistic and cultural context.

There are therefore three potential 'shocks' to the system that you are likely to experience to some degree or another. These are 'language shock', 'education shock' and 'culture shock'. These are dealt with in three separate sections in this chapter.

Be aware that going abroad for a holiday is not the same as going abroad to work or to study. The latter implies that you have to engage and to some extent confront the new cultural context that you are in. You will be challenged in terms of your identity and beliefs and therefore need to develop a way of coping and adapting. As a student you have no option but to participate in the new culture and learn the new rules of how to do things. You need to do this to fulfil the clear objective and commitment to the goals you have chosen to invest you time and money in: a useful international academic qualification and your own self-development. The stakes for you are after all quite high if you fail to adapt and that is why this section is included in the guide to explain these areas of potential shock and the necessary consideration and adaptation you will need to make. A shock to your system is best thought of as the feeling of confusion and perhaps anger when the new environment you are in is not easy to explain and understand – above all, when relying on your previous set of navigational tools and innate understandings you have developed in your home culture. Shock derives from when your expectations of how things should be done are not met. The shock comes from realising that things are different and that you are going to have to learn some new ways of understanding how things are done. Even though intellectually you may have thought this through, actual daily experience of this can be a challenging experience.

Language shock

א   आ   Ж   ح   は   艾弗   ß   !

Even though intellectually it is obvious that going to live in a new country with a new language means you are going to have to learn to communicate in a new way, the realisation that you really are going to have to do this often only occurs when you are in the new country and suddenly in a situation where you cannot make yourself understood. It is then that the enormity of the task ahead of learning a new language may hit you.

It is true that English is a world language and most people, especially the young, have a basic grasp of this language. But real misunderstanding can occur with people all the same and there is a clear need both for learning the new local language, not only for helping to get things done but also to be able to get on with local people socially.

> Learning the local language is the key to unlocking the local culture and to being able to get on with local people socially.

Learning language to get things done

We often use language to get things done. This may be to request something (e.g. you may want to buy stamps in a post office) or to explain a problem to someone (e.g. the water heater in your flat isn't working). It is soon apparent that there are key sets of vocabulary and verbs that you need to have a good grasp of for specific situations. One approach to learning this aspect of language is to note the typical situations that you need language for and to draw up a list of key vocabulary and phrases for these situations, e.g. 'language for the post office' or 'language for renting a flat'. Key to being able to learn language is being able to home in on the most useful and often used phrases for these situations. This means being able to listen to and notice what local people typically say in various situations and taking note of this. This concept means learning language items of 'high surrender value' first and not wasting time on learning words and phrases that are seldom, if ever, used.

> Surrender value = Learn language that is most useful and most used first!

It also means having a realistic understanding of how much you can learn each day. It is better to learn five key words or phrases in a day than to try and memorise a long list of words.

> Pace yourself = Do not try to learn too much at a time!

Short episodes of concentrated learning (self-testing) of five items several times a day is better than one long period of study. One technique may be to have the key words on doors, e.g. the fridge door and to have to read and self-test the items each time you open the door. Alternatively, if you are more computer dependent you can set up self-tests. There are a variety of language learning sites that you can do this from for free.

Of course learning to say things is only half the act of communicating as being able to understand what people say, especially when answering you, is also vital. Being able to predict what people are likely to say and listening out for key words helps. For example, there is little use in being able to say 'How much is this?' if you have not learnt and practised listening to numbers beforehand!

A good language learner is above all a good listener!

Learning language to be social

The other key area of language use is the social side of communicating with people. There are key phrases that you need to learn for day to day interaction with people. Being polite and showing goodwill by using appropriate language phrases is a major part of being accepted and hence living successfully in a new culture.

'Hello', 'Good morning/afternoon/evening', 'Excuse me', 'Please', 'Thank you', 'Goodbye', 'Can I have . . .?', 'Do you have . . .?' are aspects of the 'social oil' – a set stock of phrases that you need to learn for the smooth running of everyday encounters. Social language is highly cultural and the skill is to know when to use which phrases. This is called socio-linguistic competence. One of the problems is that the use of phrases and the degree to which they show respect and politeness vary greatly between cultures, which means if you say 'Please' and 'Sorry' a lot in the UK, this may not be the same for similar situations in the new culture. Conversely it may be rude to begin eating without wishing everyone present to enjoy their meal (something lacking in UK English). The best way to learn this is again to note what local people say in situations. It is then good to replicate this and notice reactions, to see if the phrase works in the situation you have used it. Using phrases successfully in context is excellent for your motivation and for remembering specific phrases.

Learning language for specific situations to get things done and to be socially successful are the first two main aspects of language that will help you settle in to the new cultural context. After this you may wish to learn language at a deeper level. This we can call 'learning language to express and explain yourself'. This involves studying the full range of the language in terms of its vocabulary and grammar. It is probably best to have the first two areas of language learnt first and in place before spending lots of time on this third aspect. In many ways this is about taking language learning beyond its 'instrumental' value and using it more in a potentially life changing 'integrative' way. This is the point where the new language and the new culture accessed by it may start to have an effect upon your world view and your sense of personal identity. Depending on who you are, some people may embrace this and other people may find this worrying.

Finally you need to think carefully about the extent to which you wish to learn to read and write the new language. There is definitely immediate payback for spending time learning to read the new alphabet. Suddenly you know which street you are in and which way it is to the next town. You feel less lost when you can read names and this can help you feel more secure in your new environment. Fortunately most languages in the world have a stronger correlation between the alphabet and the written form and the spoken sound of the written word than English (they are more phonetic). Once you have learnt the letters of the alphabet, be this in Japanese, Russian, Arabic or Spanish, you have a good idea of how the word should be pronounced, and similarly if you know how a word is pronounced you have a good idea of how it is likely to be written. Learning to decipher the alphabet and even starting to recognise written words (international brands on advertising boards are great for this) is of course very different from the task of learning to write to express yourself. Bear in mind that to be able to write a decent short essay in a foreign language you need about five years of regular daily study in that language!

> Language learning takes a long time and a lot of effort. Have realistic expectations!

The importance of learning the national language

Even if the programme you are studying on is all taught in English (it is English-medium), it is still important to learn the national language to a certain degree to at least be able to participate in the social life of the university and the city you are in. It is, of course, even more important to do so if you are able to and want to find some part-time work. Many European universities, for example, are integrated into the cities in which they are located to a greater extent than UK universities are. This means that sports clubs and cultural events are shared with the local population so that the local municipality works with the universities for this provision. The use of the national language therefore becomes even more useful to participate in the extra-curricular activities on offer. You will also come up against the local language when dealing with the inevitable bureaucracy of obtaining work permits or in contracts for renting property. Although the university should have systems in place to help its international students with these issues, knowing the local language will certainly help you understand what is going on better!

Note: Not all of the blame for not learning other languages can be laid at the door of the British. Many citizens of the world understandably enjoy the opportunity to brush up their own English when they have the chance! Remember it is all too easy to be lazy and allow this to happen, but in the end, what you really want is for the local population to teach you their language and not you to be their unofficial and unpaid English teacher, flattering as this may at first be!

Note: English language in the world: You will find that English language ability varies greatly across the world. Some countries have a very high level of English use among their population, especially among the young. This is the case in most of Scandinavia and Holland and generally the case in ex-British colonies (although this depends on the education level of the people you encounter). Eastern Europeans, certain Middle Easterners and the Chinese are leaning the language fast with the younger generations seeming particularly keen in these countries to learn and use it. Older people, however, are much less likely to be good at English and so many older, 'front of office' workers may be difficult to communicate with in English. Big language countries' populations such as those of Russia, France, Spain, China and Japan, like the British, tend to expect and rely on foreigners to use their own national languages and as a result there seems to be less widespread knowledge of English among the general population in these countries.

A further consideration is to reflect upon the fact as to whether you will be on a programme that will involve some form of work experience or placement in a local organisation or enterprise. If this is on offer or indeed an essential part of a programme of study (e.g. medicine when undertaking hospital work placements), then it is essential to learn the local language to a passable conversational level to be able to interact with patients.

It is very usual, if not expected, that universities in the EU/EEA, at least, offer free national language classes to their international students (usually as non-essential, unaccredited courses). For students going to study in Japan, Russia and China there is usually a one-year foundation programme for them that focusses on the national language and culture. The recommendation here is that full advantage is taken of these opportunities!

Education shock

Just as how we show politeness to each other varies from society to society, so do the cultural norms of how learning is deemed to best take place. There are different ideologies and approaches to learning across the world. Education systems have their own way of doing things which have been developed over many years. It is good to think of the learning context you go into as a new learning culture. This is very much about learning 'the way things get done around here' and realising they may be quite different to what you are used to. The first confusions will probably emerge around very practical issues and centre on how to find out basic information (e.g. how you are assessed, what the credit system is and what constitutes a good piece of work). Because it is basic to their own culture, the new culture you are in may assume you understand things without needing to be told!

People find it difficult to realise they need to be explicit about their own culture, and university administrations may be equally unaware of the need to make things clear to their international students!

Academic culture shock! Things to find out:

First things first:

- What are the things I need to do regarding registration?
- What is my timetable? (Where should I be and when?)
- How am I going to be taught?
- How am I going to be assessed?
- What do my tutors expect of me in terms of classroom participation?
- What is expected of me for this level of study (e.g. quantity of work)?
- Where can I get information on all of this?

And then:

- What is the structure of the programme?
- When are there holiday breaks?
- Where can I go if I am having academic issues and problems?
- What are the requirements for passing the years and the procedures for re-sits?
- What are the arrangements for using university computers and libraries?

Different approaches to knowledge and learning

You need to firstly note that the relationship between the state and the higher education system in a country is highly complex. In most countries the state defines and allocates the budget for public sector higher education and provides the legal framework for the delivery of education, examinations and evaluation. If you wonder why things cannot change for what you may feel is the better, you need to realise that universities have to follow state legislation and 'ways of acting'. You also need to be sensitive to the fact that the history of a country and its experiences has a great influence on the education you will receive and this cannot be changed easily! Private universities, unless they are seeking accreditation from the state, are consequently freer in this regard and can be more customer oriented as their reputation may depend on their clientele feeling catered for.

Perhaps a fundamental difference between university systems lies in the following: there is a continuum between those countries which are characterised by a top-down (centralised) mode of regulation, with the state having a major role in deciding the activities of a university, and at the other end of the continuum, a bottom-up (de-centralised) model where universities themselves determine their own activities and are able to make key decisions about how they are run. If you are from an educational culture that is more towards the latter, you may find it difficult to adjust to the former: you may feel that there is little opportunity for the 'student voice' to be heard by university management and for any change to be effected through student–university management consultation. (In top-down systems there may well be a tradition of student strikes as a result.) Table 2.1 shows an example of how this can vary just in Europe itself.

Key philosophies in Europe on the nature of education have been and still are the following:

1   The Humboldt tradition of the disinterested ideal of 'pure knowledge' production (academic freedom and multi-disciplinary approaches to knowledge are valued).
2   The imperial Napoleonic system (with vocational general education split from elite training. Training versus pure research are also separated).
3   The Anglo-American model of 'market forces' and the value of 'social usefulness' of education.

Influences of these three philosophies can be seen across the world and they determine very much the kind of education you will receive. As a generalisation, it is probably fair to state that there has been and is a shift occurring in countries across the world that have a highly centralised systems towards a more Anglo-American model – but this is not uniform or inevitable.

In the classroom these different philosophies will become noticeable. One big difference is that between the learner-centred approach (LCA) and the teacher-centred approach (TCA) to classroom pedagogy. This is about how learning is seen to happen and the roles and responsibilities of the teachers and learners. In the LCA, the teachers see their role as that of guide and task manager, making sure that the students undertake tasks such as mini-projects and work together on preparing presentations that they share with each other in student-led seminars. There is an emphasis on group work and group learning and on students finding out and discovering knowledge for themselves. To be effective in the LCA, the teacher needs to develop expertise in designing and 'scaffolding' activities so that students are guided in their learning, but not spoon-fed information. This they should find out themselves.

Table 2.1 Modes of regulation in Europe

Top-down centralised regulatory mode	Half-way house	Bottom-up de-centralised regulatory mode
Spain	Germany	Norway
France	Hungary	UK

Typically in the LCA, there are not so many hours of teaching time and students are expected to use library resources and undertake their own research outside of the classroom. Assessment methods often involve writing up assignments such as reports and undertaking presentations on specific agreed subjects.

In the TCA, the teaching approach is different and may involve a focus on transmitting 'received wisdom', i.e. with the teacher being the expert, teaching students what is important to know in a topic area and then expecting them to memorise this and be able to reproduce it in tests and examinations. The TCA classroom often involves more hours of class contact than the LCA and may involve more individual learning than group work. In reality, many international university classrooms may in fact be a combination of both these approaches. However, if you have been previously educated in a predominantly LCA system – characterised, for example, by a problem-based learning (PBL) approach in which you work on discovering solutions to problems – you may well find it difficult to adjust to a TCA system and vice versa.

There are advantages to both systems (TCA ensures you do not have any gaps in your knowledge – which perhaps may occur with PBL for example) and also elements of the different approaches of each may suit your own individual learning style. Knowing your own learning style preferences and your own strengths and weaknesses may help prepare you to adapt and learn better. Look at the following statements and decide which ones you are in agreement with by ticking them and then read the following commentary.

Exercise

Educational belief	Tick
1 It is the job of the teachers to be experts in the subjects they teach and to tell students what they need to know.	
2 The main job of a teacher is to show students how to discover ideas for themselves and to give them the opportunity to do so.	
3 There are no right and wrong answers to questions: facts are not fixed but rather interpretations. 'Correct' answers are therefore, in reality, simply good arguments.	
4 It is the job of students to listen to teachers' ideas, take notes from the teachers, learn the ideas and then repeat them in exams.	
5 Learning is about being given the right facts and memorising them.	
6 The real aim of a university education is to show students how to find things out rather than to tell them what to know.	
7 When students fail a course it is because they do not work hard enough.	

Educational culture note: Depending on the education you have received so far in your life (the educational culture you have experienced), you will have developed certain views and expectations about learning and teaching and yours and your teachers' roles concerning this.

Commentary: If you have ticked any of the following boxes, 1, 4, 5, then your beliefs are for a traditional approach to learning – criticised in some quarters as the 'jug and glass method' – with the teacher being a jug pouring water (knowledge) into an empty glass (the student). Many UK teachers do not believe in this approach and conceive of learning as something that should occur when learners are active themselves and seek their own knowledge. This is based also on the belief that a learner is never an empty glass and that the knowledge a learner already has is important to build on. In a more progressive education there may also not exist the belief that there is a right set of answers to everything but rather that there are many possible different right answers to questions. If you are of a more traditional outlook you may find that progressive approaches seem to lack rigor and hard work – appearing to their critics to be a bit 'wishy-washy'.

If you have ticked boxes 2, 3 and 6 then you are probably more in tune with a progressive philosophy of education. If you enter a more traditional educational setting, therefore, you will need to adapt and accept that more weight is put upon memorisation and rote learning of facts. It is true that some subjects seem to offer themselves better to the 'right and wrong answer' approach: natural science subjects and medicine may seem to lend themselves more to this – but of course, if that were the whole story, there would be no advances and no new research being undertaken to make advances! The history of science and medicine is that of proving current theories wrong. This is not to say that basic facts need to be rediscovered in each class, but that a spirit of critical thinking and enquiry does need to be developed in all learners for future progress in the discipline to occur.

Learning strengths and weaknesses test

Look at the following learning skills and decide which ones you are good at and that come naturally to you and which ones you are not so good at and may need to work on:

Exercise

Learning strength/weakness	*Good (✓)*	*Bad (✓)*
1 Concentrated listening to others presenting facts and figures		
2 Interactive discussion with others about points of view		

Learning strength/weakness	Good (✓)	Bad (✓)
3 Memorising facts and figures for examination purposes		
4 Finding out information by myself and using this in my work		
5 Taking and organising my lecture notes and learning materials		
6 Revising facts and figures and self-testing these effectively		
7 Securing and reading the set texts in time for lessons		
8 Summarising the main points from information presented to you		
9 Sharing, discussing and checking learning points from class with other students		
10 Contesting and discussing points made by the other members of the class including the lecturer		

If you are used to a LCA and have done well in such an approach, you are probably familiar with and good at 2, 4 and 9 already. If you have been trained in a TCA you are probably good at 1, 3, 6 and 8. For both approaches to learning you will need to have developed good organisational skills (5 and 7) to survive and do well. In fact, all of these skills are useful ones to develop and so it is sensible to realise which ones you are weaker at and need to work on, especially if they are skills that are valued and rewarded in the new educational culture you have come in to. Particularly important in terms of cultural etiquette is point number 10. In a LCA, the teacher may encourage students to question publicly and venture their opinions in class. This, however, may not be seen as constructive or understood in a more TCA. It may even be felt to be disrespectful and disruptive by the lecturers and other local students more used to a TCA. It is best to check what the normal classroom behaviour is before assuming this practice is acceptable.

Look at the following quote I collected from a student used to learning in a TCA culture discussing a LCA class she participated in:

When I come to class, I come to listen to the lecturer, someone who is an expert in their subject and has important points to teach me. I don't expect to have to waste my time listening to another student's half-formed and often ignorant ideas.

Thought piece: What has this student not accepted or understood about the LCA?

Of course both approaches can be done well or not so well. If you feel you simply are not learning then it may simply be because the teaching is not of a sufficient standard. The following chart may help you assess the level of teaching you are experiencing be it through a LCA or TCA.

Figure 2.2 outlines the possible kinds of teaching quality that can occur in both the LC and the TC approaches to education. In both approaches A and B are positive. In A the LCA teacher spends time preparing student activities and tasks, explains how the tasks are to be undertaken, ensures there are clear learning objectives and offers extensive feedback. On the other hand, in C, the LCA teacher abandons this responsibility and the students are very much left to fend for themselves without a clear idea of what they are learning or how they are to organise their learning. In B, the TCA teacher is knowledgeable and is able to focus student attention on the important and relevant aspects of the curriculum and explain it to them at their level. The teacher checks that students have understood the lesson. Students feel supported by the learning materials and have a clear sense of direction. In D, the TCA teacher teaches subject matter without consideration of its relevance to the students or to their level of understanding. The curriculum may appear to be a set of unconnected facts and figures. There is no checking of understanding of the lessons with the students and if a student has not understood anything it is considered to be his or her problem. There is little consideration of offering useful support materials for the learning.

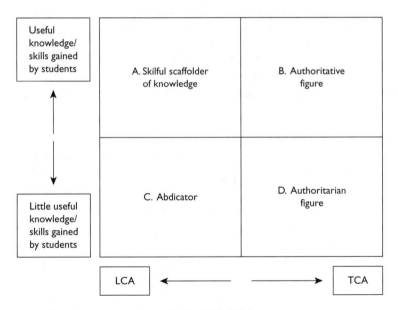

Figure 2.2 Teaching quality and the LCA/TCA.

Lesson: Bad teaching and good teaching can be a factor in both systems! Individual lecturers of course will vary in their abilities in both systems.

World approaches to education

As explained, there are fundamentally different philosophies and approaches to education existing in the world. Perhaps the biggest difference can be explained by the following concept of the 'pyramid' and 'box' approaches to university education.

Explanation: 'The pyramid'

This is a university system in which anyone with the necessary school leaving examination grades is allowed into a state university system to study. However, the process is one of 'survival of the fittest', with a high percentage of students being failed in Year 1 and in Year 2. This leads to high dropout rates as teachers spend time weeding out weak and what they consider to be non-hard working students. Students who fail usually leave with no formal qualification to show for their studies and time. Possible characteristics of the pyramid are:

- Lecture teaching mode with lecturers lecturing to hundreds of students at a time (especially in Year 1)
- Students are required to learn and not question the 'received wisdom' of the lecturer
- Little interaction between students and academic teachers
- Little group work and shared learning experiences
- An attitude that responsibility for learning rests only with the student
- Little learning support provided to the student
- Libraries tend to be small and badly furnished
- Students are expected to buy their own course books
- Student failure is seen as the students' problem

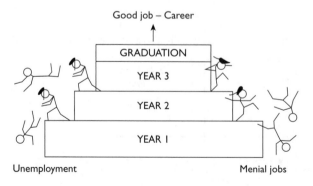

Figure 2.3 The pyramid system of higher education.

Warning! If you enter a pyramid system you may find that what is easy to enter is not necessarily easy to stay in!

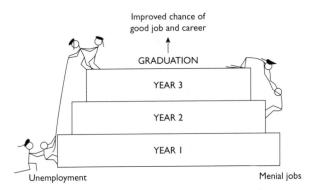

Figure 2.4 The box system of higher education.

Explanation: 'The box'

This is a system in which universities tend to control whom they select – as well as stating various entry grades, they may require interviews and use these to judge who to accept on to programmes. Once students are in the university and studying, they are monitored for signs of difficulty and study support is often recommended and provided if necessary. At the end of each year it is expected that there will be little more than 5 per cent of students 'dropping out' or failing in total (this may be seen as 'natural' attrition). Students who fail modules and hence the academic year of study can take re-sits before the next year begins to have a second chance to continue without having to repeat the year. Some universities may offer two re-sit opportunities. Universities may also offer 'concessions' for students who are ill or are experiencing other life problems. This means that these circumstances are taken into consideration and grade expectations may be adjusted accordingly. In the box system there is usually a big emphasis on library services and student support systems, as well as a system of personal tutors. There is usually also a system of diagnostic and formative testing to spot any problems students may have and be able to intervene and help them. In such systems, big lectures are not as frequent as classes, and classes tend to be small. Seminars and tutorials are also common. Teachers (academics) get to know their students and interaction between teachers and students is normal. Students are given a voice though a system of staff – student liaison meetings in which student concerns are raised and action taken at university management level.

Note: Of course education systems can be a mix of the box and the pyramid – it is unlikely that a university system is exclusively one or the other. It is also true that the more money you pay for your studies, the more likely you are to enter the box system and the less likely you are to be content with entering a pyramid system. (This helps explain the attraction for some of private universities.)

Before you enrol at an overseas university it is sensible to check the following aspects of the learning environment that are on offer. You can gather this information from the university website, prospectuses, e-mailing the university's International Office, checking out the viewpoints of current students on university Facebook pages and Student Room forums (www.thestudentroom.co.uk).

Exercise: checklist for student learning support

Aspect of support	Good (✓)	Bad (✓)
1 University library with necessary key texts in English for your subject		
2 A university intranet system that you can access with your student's code, where lecture notes and other useful support material is posted for you to access		
3 Access to teachers/lecturers to discuss any problems and issues		
4 A system of study support		
5 An international student support system		
6 An easily accessible computer system		
7 Photocopying facilities		

Notes

1   It may be expected that you have to buy the key texts yourself and that the library only stocks journals and research papers and articles. If this is the case you need to ensure you can buy these texts easily and have an idea of how much these are likely to cost each year in order to budget for this.

2   It may be that this does not exist, or if it does it may not be used extensively by lecturers. It may be that you are given handouts in class instead. In some European universities the tradition is to provide one set of handouts to a class member and expect the students to organise copying the handout amongst themselves. If this is the case make sure you understand how this works, how it is paid for and that this is indeed organised amongst the students to include you.

3   Does the university have an open door policy regarding access to lecturers when you need to check your understanding of things or have any problem and queries regarding your learning? Is there a system of tutorials built into the learning experience or are you left to fend for yourself?

4   Does the university have a support system for students who are having problems with their studies? Where can you go to talk this through?

5   Does the university have a system for supporting its international students with any problems they may be experiencing, to do with finding housing or issues to do with cultural adaptation?

6   Does the university provide computing terminals for you to use on campus, or are you expected to provide your own laptop for all your computing needs? If so, you need to check the extent of the wireless network and also which programme you need to have. You also need to check if there is technical support for you when your laptop malfunctions.

7   Does the university provide easy access to photocopy machines? It is useful if these are in the library area. If not, is it expected that you use local shops in town for this service?

Suggestion

Wherever you study it is always a good idea to set up some sort of self-help group among international students.

Culture shock

Figure 2.5 below illustrates the typical process that you as an international student may to a greater or lesser degree experience:

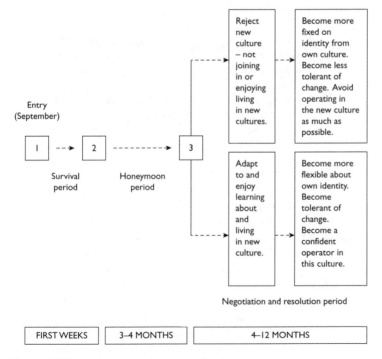

Figure 2.5 Typical stages of culture shock.

Exercise: Look at the chart and then match the stages to their explanations

Stage	Explanation
1 'Survival'	You have been in the new environment for a term/semester. You have to deal with the new culture because you are living in it. You begin to find that you are increasingly affected by the new culture and some things begin to annoy you and disorient you. You have to find a way of living in and making sense of this new culture. Some people may find this too much of a challenge and reject the new culture and decide to cling to the safety of their own culture.
2 'Honeymoon'	When you arrive at the new university you simply try to survive and have little time for analysis and reaction. You just try to be at the right place at the right time and to sort out basics such as eating and getting a place to sleep. You are focussed on the bottom rung of the pyramid of Maslow's hierarchy of needs, i.e. looking after finding solutions to the most pressing and most basic needs.
3 'Negotiation and Resolution'	Everything is new and different and this is at times curious, exciting and fun. You enjoy being away from the routine of your own culture. Even a trip to the supermarket takes on an interesting significance. However, you do not feel you yet have to really engage with the new culture in a serious way. It is still like being on holiday as a tourist.

Culture shock is a concept modelled as having distinct stages by the Canadian-born anthropologist Kalervo Oberg in the 1950s. It is now realised to be an important psychological challenge to all people who move from one cultural setting to another beyond the short term and this of course includes international students studying away from home.

There are various models of culture shock. The UK Council for International Student Affairs – UKCISA (www.ukcisa.org.uk) – is a useful website to visit as it has a section for UK students considering studying abroad. In its discussion of culture shock, UKCISA refers to five stages: the honeymoon stage, the distress stage, the reintegration stage, the autonomy stage and the independence stage. The distress stage is when the differences you encounter begin to create an impact and lead to feelings of confusion, isolation and inadequacy – a natural response to difference once the support structures of family, friends and the familiar are removed. This then leads to the reintegration stage which may involve a rejection of difference as reconnection with the home value system occurs. When in this phase, students are reminded that this is normal and that psychologically the next stage is usually the autonomy stage when differences and similarities are accepted which then leads to the independence stage when these differences are understood and become valued.

While different people, because of their different experiences and psychological makeup, vary in the degree to which culture shock has an effect upon them and the progression of the various stages, it is useful to have a general understanding and awareness of the broad phases that people can enter into as they live in another culture. Being aware of the stages may help you understand certain emotional responses to your environment that may seem to be out of character for you. Managing your way through the culture shock cycle (including knowing when you may need help with it) and being aware of what you are going through should be seen as an important part of coping with the study abroad experience.

Chapter 3

USA

Orientation

Introduction

The United States of America is commonly known by various different names, including the States, the US, the USA or simply America. The country is made up of 50 states and one federal district – Washington D.C., which is also where the capital city is located. Several other territories such as Puerto Rico and the Virgin Islands belong to the USA but are not states. The USA is a very large country both geographically and by population, traversing six time zones (including Hawaii and Alaska), and containing a population of over 300 million, making it the third most populous country in the world after China and India. It is also the fourth largest country by land area. While the populace of the USA is spread across the

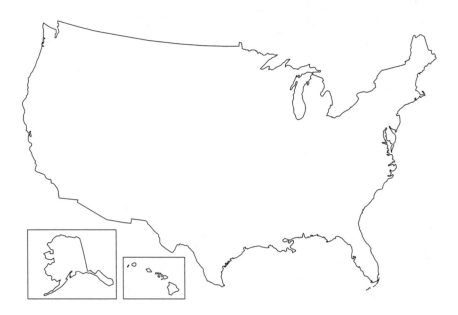

whole country, there is a greater density of its biggest cities on the East and West Coast. The largest cities in the USA by population (as listed by United States Census Bureau, 2011) are New York City (New York State) 8,250,000; Los Angeles (California) 3,800,000; Chicago (Illinois) 2,700,000; Houston (Texas) 2,150,000; Philadelphia (Pennsylvania) 1,500,000; Phoenix (Arizona) 1,500,000; San Antonio (Texas) 1,350,000; San Diego (California) 1,300,000; and Dallas (Texas) 1,200,000.

The USA is the world's largest economy, with an estimated 23 per cent of the world's total GDP. The official language of the USA is English, while Spanish is spoken by a growing number of the American population. With a large multicultural population and a culture which is familiar to many across the world through television and film, the USA is one of the most desirable places to live.

Reasons to study in the USA

- The USA is ranked in the top 15 best places to live in the world by the United Nations.
- The USA has an unparalleled reputation for academic excellence at post-secondary level, containing an incredible seven of the top ten universities in the world, and 47 of the top 100 according to the Times Higher Education World University Rankings (2012–13).
- While tuition fees in the United States are higher than in many other countries, there is a larger amount of money available for scholarships, particularly at postgraduate level.
- The privatisation of universities in the USA means that in many of the more practical degrees, universities work directly with some of the largest and most renowned companies in those fields, leading to a high incidence of employment by these companies.
- Living costs in the USA are estimated to be lower than those in the UK, particularly outside of the biggest cities such as New York or Los Angeles.
- A plethora of extra-curricular activities and societies, such as the famous fraternity system, make the university experience in the USA unique and recognisable for foreign students.

Higher education in the USA

Finding your course and institution

For both UK students, and all international students, the USA is becoming an increasingly popular destination for higher education. In 2011–12, over 9,000 UK students, out of a total of over 750,000 international students, chose to study in American universities. In California alone there were (according to the Institute of Education 2012 *Open Doors: Report on International Exchange*, www.iie.org/Research-and-Publications/Open-Doors/Data/Fact-Sheets-by-US-State/2012) more than 100,000 international students. Over half of the international students in the USA were from China, India, South Korea, Saudi Arabia or Canada. Indications are that the international student market is growing at over 5 per cent each year, with roughly half the international students enrolling for undergraduate study, while the other half are enrolled for postgraduate study. The most popular universities with international students are listed in Table 3.1.

With over 7,000 higher education institutions offering places to over 15 million students, there is an overwhelming amount of choice that confronts students looking into the possibility of studying in the USA. One of the first decisions that an international student needs to make is that of deciding which type of institution to study in. There are two principal types of higher education institutions in the USA which would be of interest to UK students: two-year institutions called community colleges or four-year institutions called universities or colleges.

Language point: Many words pertaining to the field of higher education in the USA do not correspond to their UK counterparts. The words 'college' and 'university' are used interchangeably in the USA. The word 'school' can also be used to refer to any educational institution, including universities, while in the UK it refers only to primary and secondary educational institutions. Finally, 'graduate study' is a term used in the USA to refer to what is called 'postgraduate' study in the UK, i.e. qualifications at either Master's or Doctoral level. To avoid confusion, the British terms for educational institutions and qualifications will be employed in this guide.

Community colleges

Formerly known as junior colleges, community colleges are publicly funded and offer two-year degrees known as Associate's degrees. The education on offer is broad in its nature: students will chose a major, such as Biology for example, but

Table 3.1 Most popular universities with international students

Popularity ranking	University	Number of international students 2011–12
1	University of Southern California	9,269
2	University of Illinois Urbana-Campaign	8,997
3	New York University	8,660
4	Purdue University	8,563
5	Columbia University	8,024
6	UCLA	6,703
7	Northeastern University	6,486
8	University of Michigan – Ann Arbor	6,382
9	Michigan State University	6,209
10	Ohio State University	6,142

still be expected to study a wide range of courses in, for example, History, Mathematics and Literature. In some instances, community colleges offer four-year degree programmes similar to those offered at universities. You should consult individual community college websites for information about this.

A growing number of both American and international students choose to first study at a community college, completing their first and second years there, before transferring their credits to a four-year institution. This is often possible as many community colleges have agreements with their local state universities in order to facilitate this transfer. The benefits of this approach are that community colleges are less expensive than universities, admission is non-selective and thus it is easier to get accepted on to a course. Also, as they are teaching-led rather than research-led, class sizes are smaller providing greater student support. If you are interested in studying at a community college prior to transferring to a university, make sure to check with both institutions that such a transfer is possible and that the courses you intend to study at the chosen community college will satisfy the 'core component' requirements for transfer into the chosen university.

A list of community colleges in the USA can be found at the following website: www.utexas.edu/world/comcol/state/. This provides a good place to begin your search, as you can search for them by state. This is particularly useful if you have an idea of which university you would like to transfer into, or which state you would prefer to study in.

Universities

The term university is used in this guide to broadly cover those institutions which offer degrees comparable to those offered by UK universities. However, it should be noted that there are two key differences between UK undergraduate degrees and those offered in the USA. First, while most UK degrees are three-year pro-grammes, in the USA undergraduate degrees typically last four years. Furthermore, while in the UK a high level of specialisation is available from the outset of the degree, undergraduate degrees in the USA (similarly to the Associate's degrees outlined above) are more general in nature. This means that students are required to select a 'major' as well as 'electives'. This will include, particularly in the first year, a wide breadth of subjects across both the Sciences and the Arts and Humanities.

Note: Some universities in the USA do offer 'double-major' options at under-graduate level, permitting students to study just two main subjects in greater depth. This might be of greater interest to UK students who have already begun a certain degree of subject specialisation when selecting their A levels.

While in the UK almost all universities are public, in the USA there are both private and public sector universities. Both types exist in every state. Some of the most famous, world-renowned universities are private, such as Harvard, MIT and

Stanford. However, many public universities also command a worldwide reputation, such as UCLA, Berkeley and NYU. These public universities are funded by local and state governments and usually offer lower tuition rates than private universities (this is particularly true for 'in-state' students, i.e. those originating from the state in which the university is located).

Liberal arts colleges

These are four-year private institutions, similar to universities, with a focus on undergraduate study. Their aim is to impart general knowledge and understanding, as well as to develop general intellectual capacities, as opposed to technical, professional or vocational specialisation. They are known for offering a high level of student–teacher interaction, and for having smaller enrolments and smaller class sizes. They are also famed for sometimes offering more experimental curricula than normal universities. Top liberal arts colleges, however, such as Williams College, Amherst College or Wellesley College (all in Massachusetts) are very expensive and very exclusive.

Once you have selected the type of institution you are interested in you will want to begin your search for the ideal institution and programme. Aside from the type of institutions, you should run through a mental list of all of the factors which will also be involved in your decision. You should be honest with yourself about which things are the most important for you, right down to the things that might seem most trivial. In a country as big as the USA, for example, location may well be a key consideration. You may, for example, wish to be somewhere that is easily accessible from the UK, which might limit your scope to East Coast universities, or big cities with international airports. You might be someone who is intent on living somewhere with warm weather all year round, which would rule out universities located in the northern states with harsh winters. The more honest you are about what factors are important to you, the narrower your search will become, and the easier it will be for you to find the ideal place and course. Once you have a set of criteria, a good website to begin your search is Peterson's Find-a-School Search Engine (www.petersons.com/college-search.aspx), where you can use a variety of criteria (such as location, major, tuition and others) to narrow down your search to a select list of institutions.

When you are in the process of looking at particular universities or colleges which have caught your eye, it is essential to make sure you spend time visiting their official websites. You can also try e-mailing your questions to their admissions offices, or to your particular faculty, as they are often more than willing to clear up any questions you may have. (Do make sure that you have checked the website first for the information you want, as they are unlikely to spend time outlining information which is clearly stated on their website.)

For further help investigating study options in the USA, consult both Education USA's website (www.educationusa.info/), and the US-UK Fulbright Commission's

Advisory Service. The Fulbright Commission (details below) has a centre in London and as well as holding monthly seminars it hosts a USA College Day and USA Grad School Day where useful information can be picked up.

Contact details
Telephone: 02074984010
Advisory telephone line: 09014880162
Fax: 02074984023

Mailing and visiting address
US-UK Fulbright Commission
Battersea Power Station
188 Kirtling Street
London, SW8 5BN

Website
www.fulbright.co.uk/

Opening hours
Monday: 13.30–19.00
Tuesday and Wednesday: Closed
Thursday: 13.30–17.00
Friday, Saturday and Sunday: Closed

Note: While it should not solely dictate your choice of university, it is worth understanding two important leagues of US universities: the Ivy League and the more loosely defined 'Public Ivies':

The Ivy League

This is a group of private universities (the 'Ancient Eight') in North Eastern America. The term has connotations of selectivity in admission, academic excellence and elitism. As a result of having produced a large number of successful businessmen and women (as well as many US Presidents), these universities enjoy very large endowments and have considerable financial backing. Indeed, Harvard as the richest university in the world has over $20 billion in its endowment.

Public Ivies

This is a grouping of public universities that consider themselves to be in competition to, and offering the same quality of education as, the Ivy League

Table 3.2 Ivy League universities

Institution	Date founded	Location
Harvard University	1636	Cambridge, Massachusetts
Yale University	1701	New Haven, Connecticut
University of Pennsylvania	1740	Philadelphia, Pennsylvania
Princeton University	1746	Princeton, New Jersey
Columbia University	1754	New York City, New York State
Brown University	1764	Providence, Rhode Island
Dartmouth College	1769	Hanover, New Hampshire
Cornell University	1865	Ithaca, New York

universities (this term was invented and first coined by Richard Moll (1985) in *Public Ivies: A Guide to America's best public undergraduate colleges and universities*, New York: Penguin). Table 3.3 shows the Public Ivies as organised by location.

Graduate studies

With respect to postgraduate study in the USA, there is one key difference to the UK, in that there are no pure research degrees. Master's and even Doctoral studies will always involve a mix of taught and research courses, and will also involve continuous evaluation of a student's progress. As in the UK, the price and content of postgraduate courses differs even more greatly than undergraduate courses. For this reason, it is absolutely crucial to consult individual university websites to ascertain whether the university is set up for the specific interests you have. Key considerations should be whether students have recently published in the research area you are interested in, whether the taught courses which form part of the degree are of interest to you and whether they will double up on subjects already studied at undergraduate level. You also need to check whether the university allows entry with advanced standing (if you are applying for a PhD with an MA/MSc already completed) and whether there are members of the faculty who specialise in the area you are interested in who could oversee the research you are interested in doing.

Even more than at undergraduate level, the prestige or name of the institution should not be considered as important as the individual merits each institution has in your given field. Indeed, many institutions with relatively unknown names at undergraduate level may be more well-regarded and better set up in your specific field of interest at postgraduate level than some of the more famous Ivy League institutions you have heard of.

Master's degrees

There are both Academic and Professional Master's degrees. Academic Master's offer the awards of Master of Arts (MA) or Master of Science (MSc). These

Table 3.3 Public Ivies organised by location

East Coast	West Coast	South	Mid-West
Penn State (University Park, Pennsylvania)	University of Arizona (Tucson, Arizona)	University of Florida, (Gainesville, Florida)	Indiana University (Bloomington, Indiana)
Rutgers (New Brunswick, New Jersey)	University of California, Berkeley	University of Georgia (Athens, Georgia)	Miami University (Oxford, Ohio)
State University of New York (NYC, New York State)	University of California, Los Angeles (UCLA)	University of North Carolina at Chapel Hill (Chapel Hill, North Carolina)	Michigan State (Lansing, Michigan)
University of Connecticut (Storrs, Connecticut)	University of California, Davis	University of Texas at Austin (Austin, Texas)	Ohio State (Columbus, Ohio)
University of Delaware (Newark, Delaware)	University of California, Irvine		University of Illinois (Urbana-Champaign, Illinois
University of Maryland (College Park, Maryland)	University of California, San Diego		University of Iowa (Iowa City, Iowa)
College of William & Mary (Williamsburg, Virginia)	University of California, Santa Barbara		University of Michigan (Ann-Arbour, Michigan)
University of Virginia (Charlottesville, Virginia)	University of Colorado at Boulder (Boulder, Colorado)		University of Minnesota (Minneapolis-St Paul, Minnesota)
	University of Washington (Seattle, Washington State)		University of Wisconsin (Madison, Wisconsin)

Master's can be undertaken by a thesis or non-thesis route (the non-thesis route involves taking extra taught courses). Professional Masters can be undertaken in a wide range of subjects (Business Administration, Social Work, Fine Arts, Journalism, International Relations, etc.). These, however, are often 'terminal', meaning that you cannot continue on to Doctoral programmes after them (as you are more likely able to after completing an Academic Master's degree).

Note that as in the UK, funding for Master's degree programmes is very hard to come by. Hardly any universities will offer funding to their Master's students, and any funding will have to be sought through external bodies. The US-UK Fulbright Commission has a library where funding options can be researched. US universities will often, however, provide funding for students who are going on to PhD studies. This is because MA or MSc programmes are often taken to be part of PhD programmes in the USA. For this reason, if you plan on continuing to PhD level, you should apply for PhD programmes from the start, as a Master's degree programme will be included, and funding may be provided for this if you are applying for the full PhD programme.

Doctoral programmes

As has been suggested above, funding is more readily available at Doctoral level. Most doctoral programmes, unlike the case in the UK, will involve a taught component, although if you already have a Master's degree in your chosen field, many universities will offer you advanced standing. This means that you can use courses you took at Master's degree level and receive credits for them and therefore do not have to re-do those same (or similar) courses as part of the PhD. Advanced standing will not be offered for courses taken at undergraduate level, and if you have pursued a research Master's degree in the UK, you are unlikely to receive any advanced standing at all and you will have to complete the full programme, which usually lasts five years. Note that advanced standing is usually arranged once a student is enrolled on the programme.

Accreditation

In the USA, quality control is voluntary and independent of government. There are six regional accreditation associations and one national association. These rate institutions on a range of different criteria from quality of libraries to the publications and research record of academic staff teaching in the institution.

You should be careful to check the accreditation of any institution that you are interested in applying to. If an institution makes reference to an official sounding accreditation body on their website, you should not take this at face value and assume that the institution is definitely accredited. Students are advised to check out the institution on both the US Department of Education's database and the Council for Higher Education Accreditation database, both of which can be found online.

Reasons to be initially distrustful of an institution might include: degrees being awarded in a shorter than usual time frame, a website ending in something other than '.edu', unusually flexible entry requirements, lots of recommendations from academic experts (only non-accredited 'diploma mills' are likely to try this hard sell tactic to impress prospective students), names which are similar to other famous institutions, a charge of flat rate fees instead of fees which correspond to course requirements.

The credit system

The way the academic year is divided up varies from university to university in the USA. Some universities (about 20 per cent) operate a Quarter System whereby the academic year is divided up into four blocks (one of which is an optional summer term). Otherwise a Trimester or Semester System is operated in which the year is divided either into a Fall Quarter, Winter Quarter and Spring Quarter, or is divided into two main parts. Community colleges tend to follow the high school year dates. You should be careful to make sure you understand how many academic 'blocks' you are going to go through across the length of your degree, as the credit system will require you to complete a certain number of credits to graduate. You need to be able to work out how many credits you need to take in each academic block in order to accurately pick and choose which modules to take.

One important thing to make sure you understand early on is exactly how you will be evaluated. This can differ greatly from the way it is done in the UK (i.e. based entirely around examinations at the end of the academic year). In the USA, your final grade may well be built upon things such as class participation and attendance, weekly quizzes, written papers and examinations (midterms and finals). Make sure you know whether attendance will be a decisive factor in your grades before you decide to skip a class!

Credits. Academic work is organised into modules (some of which will be mandatory and some of which will be optional). Each of these modules will take a specific amount of time (e.g. one semester) and will be valuable for a certain amount of credits, or 'credit hours'. Graduation will be dependent on the completion of a specific number of credits or credit hours (similarly transfer from one programme to another will be based upon the amount of transferable credits already taken). Most universities assign 3 credits per course, with students able to take up to 18 credits per semester. Students must usually complete 30 credits per year in order to complete their degree in the assigned time period.

Grading systems can also vary from institution to institution. Most grades will be given on an alphabetical or numerical scale (with alphabetical grades running from A–F, and numerical ones from 0–4.0). These grades will also most likely be given in fractions, allowing for grades such as a B+ or a 3.5.

To work out your GPA you need to find the average of the grades you have received across the duration of your degree, and also take into account the weighting of each module (i.e. the amount of credits which that grade was given for). For example, if you received a 3.0 (roughly equivalent to a B), in a 3-credit-module, this provides you with 9 'quality points' (3.0 x 3). If you add this to all the other quality points you have achieved, and then divide this by the total number of credits taken, you will find your GPA. Table 3.4 demonstrates the relationship between numerical and alphabetical grading systems.

You should be careful not to confuse these percentages and grades with those awarded by UK universities, where lower percentages are usually awarded. Table 3.5 shows a rough conversion of American GPAs to their UK equivalents.

Table 3.4 Relationship between numerical and alphabetical grading systems

Percentage	US alphabetical grade	US numerical grade
90–100	A+	4.33
	A	4.0
	A−	3.67
80–89	B+	3.33
	B	3.0
	B−	2.67
70–79	C+	2.33
	C	2.0
	C−	1.67
60–69	D+	1.33
	D	1.0
	D−	0.67
0–60	F	0

Table 3.5 Rough conversion of American GPAs to their UK equivalents

US GPA (numerical)	US GPA (alphabetical)	UK class	Percentage needed in UK to obtain that class
4.0	A	First class	70–100
3.0–3.33	B+/B	Upper second class	60–69
3.67–3.0	B/B−	Lower second class	50–59
2.0	C	Third class	40–49
1.0	D	Pass	30–39
0	F	Fail	0–30

Note: As well as your grades, there are some other means by which US universities distinguish between their students. First, it is common among American universities to rank students by their GPA, allowing for students to be within the *n*th percentile in their class. The 'valedictorian' is the student with the top GPA, while the 'salutatorian' is the student with the second highest GPA. Furthermore, many institutes confer different levels of Latin honours on graduates:

Translations of Latin honours titles:

- *'Cum laude'* means 'with honour'
- *'Magna cum laude'* means 'with great honour'
- *'Maxima cum laude'* means 'with very great honour'
- *'Summa cum laude'* means 'with highest honour'
- *'Egregia cum laude'* means 'with outstanding honour'

Financing your studies

Tuition fees and living costs

Tuition fees

In the USA, tuition fees are set by individual institutions. As the higher education sector is market driven there exists great variety between the amount charged by each institution. The tuition fees paid by international students are, however, across the board, considerably higher than that paid by 'resident' or 'in-state' students, i.e. those from the local area. This is particularly noticeable in public universities.

Various estimates put the average yearly tuition fees for an international student at undergraduate level at around $20,000 per year for public institutions, and around $30,000 per year at private institutions. There is, however, a great deal of variation from university to university, and it is worth consulting each individual university's websites for up to date, accurate information about their fees. It is also worth bearing in mind that while some of the more prestigious and famous universities, such as those in the Ivy League, may have the highest tuition fees, they are also the ones that operate the most generous scholarship and funding programmes, and so may end up being comparative or even cheaper in price than other universities who offer lower tuition fees but have no funding available for students. Harvard University is a good example, as they operate a 'need blind' admissions policy based purely on academic merit. Currently, students who fit the bill academically, but whose parents have a combined income of less than $65,000 have their fees covered by the university.

If you are considering the community college route it is also worthwhile noting that tuition fees at a community college can be as little as $3,000 per year, making it a very attractive option economically speaking.

Once again there is even greater variety at postgraduate level. As has already been suggested, Master's studies in the USA are likely to be very expensive, with programmes lasting two years and costing as much as $30,000 per year and with no funding available. PhD students, however, are likely to find some of their tuition covered by funds available from the universities themselves, while some go as far as to cover all tuition and provide a living stipend for Doctoral students to be able to focus on their research.

Living costs

Aside from tuition fees, you need to consider the price of living in the USA while pursuing your studies. You should add these costs to your tuition fees to work out a rough estimate for how much it will cost in total per year to study in the USA. UCLA, for example, estimates a total of $55,000 per year. Table 3.6 details the rough costs of living in the USA. For more detailed information consult the 'Student life in the USA' section below.

Table 3.6 Cost of living in the USA

Cost	Price
Application fees	American universities charge application fees from those applying. This fee can vary from around $30 to as much as $100. One should plan on applying to around four or five universities and thus set aside around $300 as a minimum for application fees.
Accommodation	Including accommodation and food, your living costs should be no more than around $12,000–15,000 per year. This will of course depend on what type of accommodation you opt for and how much you eat out, etc. See the 'Student life in the USA' section for more detailed information.
Extra living costs	You should bear in mind that you will have other costs such as gym membership, running a mobile phone, etc. An estimate of $500 per year for extra necessary miscellaneous costs is advised.
Books and supplies	The price of purchasing all the relevant materials for studying can be high in the USA, and as much as $800 might be needed to purchase all the necessary materials for your course.
Health insurance	As there is no National Health Insurance in the USA, this is a key consideration. Indeed, to be issued with a J-1 visa, the university needs proof of the student having some form of health plan. Many universities will offer their own plans, which vary in quality. Similarly, price will vary between different university cover plans, and those offered privately. You can expect to pay up to around $3,000 per year for comprehensive health insurance.
Transport costs	You should also consider transportation. Many students in the USA run vehicles while at university, and if you choose to do so you will have to factor in this extra cost. If you live in a metropolitan area you might choose to use public transport. In this case you should factor in monthly transport passes (a monthly student pass in LA, for example, is $24).

Financial aid

As stated above, students enrolling at American universities will find that there are often scholarships or funding opportunities provided by the universities themselves. In fact, 25 per cent of students studying in the USA have their main source of funding as the university they have enrolled in. Doctoral programmes are those which usually have the greatest amount of funding available, while Master's degree programmes are those which tend to have least. Scholarships can be based on an academic, sports or needs basis. For information regarding funding available at the university itself it is important to contact the university directly. This is particularly important as some universities will require you to fill out separate applications for sources of funding, while at others all applicants will automatically apply for funding opportunities.

It is important to note that most university funding will be renewable on a year or semester basis, meaning that students will be required to keep their GPA at a specified standard to continue receiving the scholarship.

Outside the university, there are other sources of potential funding available. The key to funding your studies in the USA is to look for multiple sources of funding and start your research early. The Fulbright Awards Programme is an organisation which offers scholarships for academic work in any subject, at any accredited US university. Approximately 30 scholarships are offered each year to UK citizens for the first year of postgraduate or Doctoral study, or for 'special research'. These scholarships cover tuition fees and provide a living stipend for one academic year. The competition for these awards opens on 1 August with an application deadline of 15 November. Interviews are then organised for January or early February.

Outside of the scholarships they offer, the US-UK Fulbright Commission is a good place to start your search for external sources of funding. To give yourself the best chance of finding the funding you need, you should start your research as early as a year to a year and a half before you intend to start your chosen course.

Student loans

Unless you have American citizenship, or dual citizenship between the USA and another country, it is not possible to obtain a US student loan. However, if you have a creditworthy US citizen or permanent resident who is willing to co-sign the loan with you, then students without US citizenship may be able to apply for loans.

In the former case, loans can be applied for via the Federal Student Aid's website (www.fafsa.ed.gov). These federal loans tend to offer low interest rates and allow deferred repayment due to their status as a 'student loan'.

In the latter case, your university will usually be able to inform you of local banks and other lenders you can approach in order to secure a loan. Note that these loans are likely to have higher interest rates than those offered to US citizens, but they are still classified as 'student loans'. If you do decide to take out a loan and meet the conditions stipulated by the lender, compare the terms and conditions of multiple loans offered and make sure you know exactly what is expected of you before you sign up for a loan of this type.

Application procedure

There are various criteria used by US universities to determine which students they accept on to their programmes. They are likely to take into consideration the following:

1   Results at secondary school level (or post-secondary level for graduate applicants).
2   Scores on mandatory standardised tests (e.g. SAT for undergraduate, or GRE for postgraduate applicants).
3   Essays (either one previously submitted at your last institution, or in some cases, one written specifically for the application).
4   Recommendation letters from teachers, or academic references in the case of postgraduate applicants.
5   Extra-curricular activities (a demonstrated active interest in fields pertaining to your academic subject area is taken into strong consideration).

Time frame

Universities in the USA operate to strict application deadlines, so the first thing you need to do when you have narrowed down your list of institutions is check the application deadlines on their websites and compile a list so that you don't miss any. Most application deadlines fall in the months of December, January or February, and decisions will usually be published in the late spring.

A lot of work needs to be done before the application deadlines, as there are many documents that need gathering and research that needs to be undertaken. This is particularly true of postgraduate students, or students who are searching for sources of external funding. You should thus begin the application process as early as a year before you intend to begin your chosen course.

Application fees

As there is no equivalent in the USA to the UCAS system in the UK, you will usually apply directly to each university you wish to apply to. These institutions normally require a non-refundable application fee, which tends to be somewhere between $30–100. This can usually be paid by credit card on the university website. A receipt of this payment is needed for you to send off the online application form.

This is one reason, among others, to keep the number of institutions you are applying to down to somewhere between four and six. It is up to you whether you choose universities of differing academic rankings in order to try and secure backup universities for yourself, or whether you only choose to apply to a select number of universities which you would be prepared to travel abroad to study at.

Note: There is something called the Common Application, which offers a way of making multiple applications at once. Over 240 colleges and universities use this system. It involves downloading the application form from http://common app.org/ and sending it to any of the participating universities you are interested in applying to. It is free, but be sure to check that the universities you are interested in are listed on the website as participating institutions.

High school transcripts or university transcripts

Different grading systems in the USA at both secondary and university level mean that there are some difficulties in understanding what is needed for an application. American schools and universities work on the basis of continuous assessment, meaning that they tend to ask for transcripts detailing the grades and subjects studied over the whole course of students' school or university careers. However, in the UK academic records tend to be based solely on final exams, either at the end of each year or sometimes only at the end of a whole degree or qualification.

One way to get round this is to list previous results along with those achieved most recently. For example, students applying to undergraduate programs may want to list GCSE and AS Level results along with A Level results to provide a fuller picture of their secondary school career. Similarly you might choose to list results achieved in any Preliminary Examinations taken during your university career along with your final results. Appendix 1 at the end of this guide provides a useful model for you to use for sending in your high school transcript.

Ultimately, however, this is not something to worry too much about. Most institutions in the USA will be familiar with the UK system and will understand the results listed on your application. Do not try to calculate what your GPA 'would have been' based on your A Level, IB or BA/BSc results, just stick with the qualifications as they are given in the UK. If you have any doubts about this contact the university directly to ask how to present your results.

Standardised examinations

SATs and ACTs

As well as your secondary school results, most American universities require you to present your results from a standardised test along with your application. At undergraduate level this will be the SATs or in some cases the ACTs. It is important for you to note that standardised exams are important to do, not only because they are used to determine whether students are offered a place, but they are also used to determine the recipients of university funding.

Make sure to check with all of the universities you are going to apply to which one, if either, of these standardised exams is needed. These examinations need to be taken at least a month before the application is due (SATs, for example, are only available to view within 17–20 days of sitting the exam), but taking them even earlier may be a good idea as it allows time for a re-take.

Some universities may require you to take the SAT subject tests as well as the standard SAT reasoning test. The SAT subject test lasts one hour and is a multiple choice paper, while the SAT reasoning test lasts over three and a half hours includes reading, writing and mathematics. Your score in your SAT subject test will be between 200–800, while your score in the SAT reasoning test will be between 600–2,400 (comprised of three scores of 200–800: reading, writing and mathematics). You will also be given a 'percentile', which locates your score among all other students who took the test that day.

The SAT reasoning test is given seven times a year, while the individual SAT subject tests are given six times a year. The ACT is held five times a year. Once you have registered for the SAT on the College Board Website (http://sat.college board.org/home), you can choose four institutions for your SAT results to be sent to. If you want to wait to see how you have done, you can log into your account on the website at a later date and choose the universities then. For each university over the four you can send your results to, you must pay an additional $10.50. The fee for sitting the SAT is variable, and is best found on the College Board website.

GREs and GMATs

As with undergraduate programmes, postgraduate programmes in the USA usually require standardised examination results along with undergraduate results. Even when applying for programmes in specialised subject areas, including at Doctoral level, universities will usually ask for at least the standard GRE (for humanities) or GMAT (for business schools). As with SATs, there are subject tests available at GRE level, although these are required less often.

The GRE measures your verbal reasoning, quantitative reasoning, critical thinking and analytical writing skills – skills that are not related to a specific field of study, but which are considered important for all. The results for these sections are scored on a 130–170 scale for verbal and quantitative reasoning, and on a 0–6 half-point scale for analytical writing. The test takes 3 hours and 45 minutes and can be taken at computer-based centres in Birmingham, Edinburgh, London, Manchester and Peterborough.

As with the SATs, you can have your results sent directly to the universities you are applying to. Students can re-take the test if necessary, up to five times in one 12-month period. The results are valid for up to five years from the date you sat the exam. It is, however, a good idea to keep the number of times you sit the exam down to a minimum, as it costs $175 to sit.

Students can register for the GRE test at the following website: www.ets. org/gre/revised_general/register/

Visa information

The most common visa for students to study in the USA is the F-1 visa. The only cases in which you would not be issued with this type of visa are ones where the student is enrolling on a one-year vocational programme (M-1), or where the student is an exchange student and needs to undergo practical training as part of the course (J-1). In all cases, the university you are enrolling at will determine which type of visa you need.

Applying for the F-1 visa

For most undergraduate and postgraduate programmes, if you are made an offer, the university will send you an I-20 form. This will be sent once the university is satisfied that you have the necessary finances to complete your studies. The I-20 form acts as a Certificate of Eligibility for Non-immigrant (F-1) Student Status.

Once you receive your I-20 you need to check that your details are correct on the Student and Exchange Visitor Information Service (SEVIS). SEVIS is an internet database which tracks all students and exchange visitors and can be found at the following website: www.ice.gov/sevis/. Your details will have been registered on this website by your sponsor, i.e. by your university or college. Once you have checked that your details are correct, you will need to pay the SEVIS (1-901) fee. This can be done at www.FMJfee.com by completing the online 1-901 form and paying by credit or debit card. The fee is currently $200 for F-1 visas. You should keep the receipt for this payment.

The next stage for UK students is to apply for the actual visa. This should be done at either the US Embassy in London (24 Grosvenor Square) or the US Consulate General in Belfast (Danesford House, 223 Stranmillis Road). To make an appointment you have to call the Operator Assisted Information and Non-immigrant Visa Appointment Booking Service on Tel: 0942 450 100.

At your interview you will need to show the following documentation:

1   An I-20 form.
2   Proof of SEVIS fee payment.
3   A valid passport.
4   A completed visa application form DS-160, available from the following website: https://ceac.state.gov/genniv/.
5   Documents showing sufficient funds for first year tuition fees and living costs and evidence of a means to pay for the rest of the years.
6   Passport sized photographs.

After your interview your visa should be processed in five to seven days, although if further investigations are deemed necessary, it can take up to 90 days.

Visa application timeline

It is advised that you start your visa application process as quickly as possible, and start dealing with your SEVIS fee payment as soon as you receive your I-20 from your chosen institution. The earliest you can apply for your actual visa, however, is 120 days before the registration date for the course you intend to study.

Once you have your visa you can begin to organise your travel arrangements, but you should note that you can only enter the USA on your F-1 visa 30 days or less before your registration date. UK citizens can, however, enter the USA on a travel visa prior to this if more time is deemed necessary.

You should carry your visa and I-20 with you when entering the country, as well as your I-94 (Arrival–Departure Record) which is used as proof of legal entry into the country.

Student life in the USA

Campus life

American universities offer students a wide variety of activities, sports and societies which they can get involved in throughout the course of their studies. Sport plays a major role on US campuses, and you will find that university (American) football, basketball and baseball games are important social events for all students. There are usually three levels of sporting participation on campuses: intercollegiate, whereby the top university varsity teams compete with other universities (these are NCAA league games and are often televised); intramural, whereby teams from within the same university compete with one another; and recreational, whereby students get together to play sports in order to have fun and stay in shape. This wide variety of levels means that students are able to participate in different sports regardless of their ability. Students will also find that although US sport revolves principally around American football, basketball, ice hockey and baseball, sports of all different types are practised by students at university in the USA, and students should be able to find a club or society for their sport of choice. Indeed, in recent years football (soccer) has become increasingly popular in American schools and universities.

Outside of sports, students will find that there are a wide variety of associations and societies to match their interests and vocations. Religious freedom is also absolute in the USA and most campuses have facilities for practising the range of faiths that make up the cosmopolitan population of modern universities.

Many universities offer fraternities (for men) and sororities (for women). These are organisations named after Greek letters and are comprised of groups of students who share common interests and want to socialise together. The tradition of fraternities and sororities dates back as far as the 1770s, and the oldest active fraternity is the Kappa Alpha Society, which was founded in 1825. The image of fraternities and sororities has become popularised in many films and TV shows, and have gained an image of being particularly wild. However, many are in fact quite conservative in nature and this should not be taken as the general widespread reality.

For students wishing to involve themselves in American university campus culture, joining a fraternity or sorority may be something which might be attractive. It can also provide a good opportunity for students to meet other like-minded students, and particularly to meet other American students. Students should note, however, that fraternities and sororities can also be expensive, as students often have to pay 'dues' which can vary a lot in price. These are used to cover the facilities which the fraternity or sorority offer, such as meal plans, group trips or other facilities.

Accommodation and student living

Depending on where the university is located and on personal preferences, students will choose to live either in university accommodation or privately rent a property. Universities usually offer campus residence halls (also known as dormitories) to their students, where you will share bathroom, laundry and kitchen facilities with other students. These dormitories have resident advisors (usually one on each floor) who are able to assist students with any problems they may have. Dormitories can be a good, and safe, option for students during their first year of university, as they are usually located either on campus or within a short distance from campus. Dormitories may also provide a good option for students upon arrival in America as they put students in immediate regular contact with other students in their position. However, it should be noted that unlike in the UK, in the USA students usually share rooms in university dormitories with one other student. Prices of dormitories can also vary greatly, so it is worth contacting your university beforehand to check, although average prices tend to be around $8,000 per year.

You may thus chose to live in dormitories for your first year, or even just for a short period upon arrival, while searching for private accommodation. Students living in big metropolitan cities may in fact choose to go straight into private accommodation, or may find that their university does not have sufficient student housing for all its students. When searching for private accommodation it is a good idea to contact the housing office or student's union at the university or college at which you study, as they will often be able to provide information about where to find accommodation, which areas are the best to live in and what prices you can expect to pay.

The rent you can expect to pay will vary greatly depending on a variety of factors, including whether you share with other students, the quality of accommodation, and the area of the city, and indeed area of the country, where you intend to live. As a general example, certain big cities such as New York and San Francisco have a reputation for being the most expensive cities in America, while you will find that in general, cities in the centre of the country cost less than those on either seaboard.

Health insurance

All international students wishing to study in the USA will need to take out private health insurance. Healthcare in the USA can be extremely expensive and any international students who do not have health insurance will be expected to pay privately for any healthcare they may need while in the country. It is therefore essential for students to have health insurance before going to study in the USA. Indeed, the US Government requires all students on J-1 visas to have health insurance, while students on F-1 visas are usually required to have health insurance by the university they plan to attend.

Many colleges and universities, particularly the larger ones, will have health plans for their international students, and information about each of these can be found on the individual university or college websites. Participation in a university or college health plan is often mandatory. Students who are being sponsored for their studies by an organisation such as USAID or one of the Fulbright programmes may find that the organisation has its own health insurance policy for the students who go through it. Similarly, graduate students receiving funding from their university for their Master's degree or PhD programme will often find that their health insurance is covered within the funding they receive. In either case, it is very important that students make sure that they are not only covered, but are familiar with what is included in their policy before going out. The following definitions should help students get their head around their health insurance policy:

Premium	This is the amount you pay to purchase your health insurance.
Deductible	This is the minimum amount the insured person needs to pay before the insurance company pays the rest of the costs for any type of treatment or healthcare.
Co-insurance	This is the percentage of any further costs above the deductible which is still paid by the insured person. For instance, if the co-insurance is 20 per cent, then the student will still need to pay 20 per cent of any costs above the deductible, with the insurance company paying the remaining 80 per cent.
Expenses	Some expenses may not be covered within the health insurance policy, and students need to be aware of these. Students should make sure they are familiar with any expenses which they will be expected to cover themselves.

Whether or not the university or college you are planning to attend provides a health plan for students, you are advised to contact the International Office at your chosen institution to get advice about which policy is recommended for international students.

Students who are not having their health insurance covered for them through any sort of funding can expect to pay roughly between $1,800–3,000 for health insurance per year. This will depend on the type of cover you opt for and which university you are studying at. It is advisable for students to try and get the most extensive health insurance offered by the university in order to avoid any nasty surprises further down the line.

Work while you study

There are sometimes options available for international students who want to work part-time while studying to bring in a little extra money to help with costs. It should be advised, however, that students are not permitted to rely on their salary from part-time work to support themselves, and any money gained from part-time employment should be viewed as supplementary to their main source of income.

The easiest option for students is to work on campus, as this does not need approval from the United States Citizenship and Immigration Service (USCIS). Work on campus will often be harder to come by, however, and at most universities will require the authorisation of the International Office, who will often not grant permission to students in their first term, or even year. Students who do work on campus will only be able to do so up to a maximum of 20 hours per week during term time, and 40 hours per week during vacation periods.

Students may be permitted to work off campus for up to 20 hours per week during term time, and 40 hours per week during vacation periods, under what is defined as 'severe economic hardship'. Students will need to be performing well academically, and must be able to show that they are currently under severe economic hardship. Furthermore, this new lack of funding must be proven to be due to unforeseen circumstances (meaning students cannot plan on having access to this extra work before beginning their degree).

Outside of these options, international students may be able to do internships or work for up to one year in a field related to their studies alongside their degree. This can be done with a recognised international organisation, or through the Optional Practical Training (OPT) or Curricular Practical Training (CPT) programmes. Students interested should seek more information about these options from their universities once they have enrolled on their programme.

Further practical information

Transport

International students may plan on running a car while they are studying in the USA, particularly if they are not living in a major city or are studying at a campus university. UK drivers can drive in the USA for up to one year on their UK Driving Licence, or with an International Driver's Permit (IDP). After this students will be required to obtain a local driving licence in the state where they are residing. This, along with other costs such as insurance, repairs and the initial cost of purchase, will need to be carefully considered by students, as running a car can push your budget up considerably. On the plus side, however, UK students will find that the price of gasoline in the USA is considerably cheaper, with a gallon costing US$3.29 according to the Bloomberg Gas Price Ranking (2013), as compared to US$8.06 back home.

It may work out considerably cheaper for students to choose to use public transport while living in the USA. This is particularly true of students living in major cities with well integrated local transport systems. Monthly or even yearly passes are available in most major cities, and can cost between $30–120 per month. The following is a list of the costs of a monthly transit pass in the major US cities: New York City ($112), Los Angeles ($75), Chicago ($100), Philadelphia ($83), Phoenix ($64), Houston ($38.60), San Antonio ($35), San Diego ($72), Dallas ($80). Note that in some states international university students are able to benefit from discounted rates. For more information you should contact your university or the local transit authorities to find out what pass will best suit your needs.

Banking

International students will find that owning an American bank account while studying in the USA will make life considerably easier. This is particularly true of students receiving funding or a living stipend, as this can be paid directly into their American bank account. Opening a bank account in the USA will also avoid students being charged for withdrawing money.

Universities themselves may have a relationship with a particular local bank, and it is worth asking the International Office at the university you are studying at about where to open a bank account. Students will most likely need a combination of their passport, university ID, visa and I-20/I-94 in order to be able to open an account. Students are advised to check whether there are any specific student accounts offered by any banks local to where they are studying, as these can also include added benefits for international students.

Mobile phones

There are many different network providers across the USA, and different providers will operate in different areas. To find out which provider is best in the area you are planning to study, it is best to consult with other local students once you have arrived.

International students may choose to go for a pay-as-you-go deal in order to avoid being tied down to a contract. If students do opt for a monthly plan, this could cost in the region of $25 per month (depending on the network provider and the terms and conditions of your package).

After you finish your degree

For students wishing to stay on in the USA, there are only a couple of options available to them. If they are on an F-1 visa they may be able to stay on for one year after graduation. However, this is only in the case of graduates of particular subjects who are able to do specific training related to their degree. Students should consult with their university to see whether this option may be available to them upon graduation.

Otherwise, students intending to remain in the USA after completion of their degree will need to have a job offer from a company wishing to sponsor their visa application. Companies willing to sponsor visa applications tend to be larger firms, and they tend to only sponsor applications for more specialised positions where it would be harder to find many other people who would be able to perform the job. That said, it will be easier for international students studying at an American university to find a company willing to sponsor their visa application than it would be for students based abroad who are trying to do so from across the Atlantic. High-performing students graduating from American universities should not be put off by the idea of trying to find employment in the USA which will allow them to carry on after graduation.

Those students who do not choose to remain in the USA upon graduation from their degree will find themselves competitive, not only back in the UK, but in the international job market. The quality of American higher education is recognised worldwide as being very high, and having studied abroad has the added benefit of having internationalised your CV. Similarly, students who wish to continue on in higher education will find themselves in a good position to apply for Master's degree or PhD programmes at other universities worldwide, as their US degree will put them in a strong position for consideration.

Whatever students go on to do after completing their studies in the USA, they should be able to look back on a fantastic university experience, and look forward to a myriad of opportunities ahead of them.

Chapter 4

Canada

Orientation

Introduction

Canada is the world's second largest country, traversing six time zones from the Newfoundland to the Pacific coast. Despite this huge expanse of land, the population of Canada is smaller than the UK, totalling just 32 million Canadians. One of the principal reasons for this is the extreme weather conditions, making

much of the north of the country uninhabitable. For this reason, a large part of the population lives in areas along the southern border of the country with the USA. This is where the majority of Canada's largest cities are located, with the largest in population being Toronto (Ontario) 2,615,000; Montreal (Québec) 1,649,000; Calgary (Alberta) 1,096,000; Ottawa (Ontario) 883,000; Edmonton (Alberta) 812,000; Mississuaga (Ontario) 713,000; Winnipeg (Manitoba) 663,000; and Vancouver (British Columbia) 578,000.

English and French are the official languages in Canada, with around 7 million native French speakers living in Québec which was a French colony. Universities in Québec often run their programmes in French, and the region has a high level of autonomy and thus application procedures can be very different for universities in Québec. Across the whole country, however, English is the primary language, and is spoken by roughly 75 per cent of the population as the native tongue.

Canada is one of the world's wealthiest nations and despite its relatively small population commands the tenth largest economy in the world. It is ranked as one of the best places to live in the world by the United Nations and enjoys a very high standard of living.

Reasons to study in Canada

- Canada is ranked by the United Nations as one of the best places to live in the world.
- Canada is a politically stable, multicultural and safe country to study in; it was ranked as the eighth safest country in the world in the 2013 Global Peace Index (www.visionofhumanity.org/pdf/gpi/2013_Global_Peace_Index_Report.pdf).
- Tuition fees in Canada are lower on average than comparable courses offered in the UK, the USA, New Zealand and Australia.
- Comparatively low living costs further emphasise the value for money of a Canadian degree.
- There is the possibility to work while studying through certain programmes offered by Canadian universities.
- The quality of education in Canada is internationally recognised to be of a very high level and is highly regulated by the state, guaranteeing its validity.
- After having completed a degree in a Canadian university there are structures in place to allow students to remain in the country for work after graduating through certain visa programmes.

Higher education in Canada

Finding your course and institution

There are more than 100,000 international students who choose to study in Canada each year; of these, 1,100 are UK students. There is a wide array of different universities in Canada, offering 10,000 different programmes across the country. There is a huge amount of choice and difference from university to university. Education in Canada is the responsibility of individual provinces and districts, and therefore standards and requirements vary from province to province and district to district. This aside, the majority of institutions in Canada are state funded, and there are relatively few private universities in Canada compared to its neighbour the USA.

An early decision that needs to be made is as to what type of institution you wish to study at. The Association of Universities and Colleges of Canada (AUCC), an organisation composed of Canadian universities, defines two distinct types of post-secondary institutions in Canada: universities and colleges. Universities grant university degrees, which include Bachelor's, Master's and Doctoral degrees; and colleges, also known as community colleges, provide diplomas.

Universities

There are just under 100 independent post-secondary education institutions with degree-granting authority in Canada. The oldest is the Université Laval in Québec, while the largest is the University of Québec itself with 87,000 students. The qualifications gained at Canadian universities are degrees comparable to those which are studied for at UK institutions. The academic year usually starts in September and ends in May as it does in the UK, being comprised of two semesters (although some universities do operate a trimester system). However, generally across Canada an undergraduate degree is of four years in duration, compared to the three years in the UK.

Colleges

Aside from universities, you may wish to investigate colleges in Canada. There are around 150 colleges in Canada, which are similar in ethos to the US community colleges, although they do not usually award Associate's degrees. (Unlike in the USA, colleges in Canada refer to non-academic degree awarding institutions, such as practical work oriented qualifications.) In Québec, these colleges are referred to as 'Cégeps'. One popular option with students are the colleges in British Columbia which offer university transfer programmes and US style Associate's degrees that allow for transfer into year three of university programmes. For more information consult www.bccolleges.ca/.

Once you have chosen which type of institution you are interested in studying at, you will want to begin your search for the right course and institution. There will be many factors involved in your decision, and it is a good idea to make a list of things that are important to you, in terms of both what type of course you wish to do, as well as where you want to live. For example, it might be important to you to live in a big lively city, or you may be someone who prefers smaller towns. Making a checklist of this nature is important, as the more points you have, the more universities and courses will be ruled out leaving you with your ideal institution and programme.

As with location, programme and price are likely to be key factors in the decision-making process and a good place to begin your search is The Association of Universities and Colleges of Canada (www.aucc.ca/canadian-universities/our-universities). The Association represents 96 institutions, and the website is a good place to begin as you can search through the universities, organising them by course, location and tuition fees. When searching for universities, it is important to remember that in Québec, all universities apart from McGill University (Montréal), Concordia University (Montréal) and Bishop's University (Lennoxville) are French-language, while those listed previously are the only English-language universities in Québec.

Note: While university rankings are by no means the be-all-and-end-all of your search for the perfect university course, it may be worthwhile considering that according to the Times Higher Education World University Rankings (2012–13), five Canadian universities are in the top 100: University of Toronto (21st), University of British Columbia (30th), McGill University (34th), University of Montreal (84th) and McMaster University (88th).

The credit system

Because of the devolved nature of the education system in Canada, there is a lot of diversity with regards to the credit and grading systems. However, in essence the system is similar to that in the USA. Universities award credit hours with the norm being 3 credit hours per course per semester. Your GPA will be calculated by looking at your grade (e.g. B or 3.0), multiplying this by the number of credit hours for the course and adding it to the totals for other courses. This is then divided by the total number of credit hours you have taken. Although it varies, in Canada you often fulfil 30 credits per year, totalling 120 over the four years of undergraduate study.

While a usual GPA is out of a maximum of 4.0 like it is in the USA, some systems in Canada base their GPA on a nine-point scale. In general, it does not make any difference what you are scored out of. It is essential that you make sure you contact the university and understand the credit system that they operate so that you know how many credits you need to obtain each year and don't find yourself falling short.

Financing your studies

Tuition fees and living costs

Tuition fees

Tuition fees in Canada are set by individual institutions. They vary dependant on the institution and the course offered, but are often better priced than equivalent programmes in the USA, the UK, Australia and New Zealand. In 2011, tuition fees averaged C$16,000 (£10,000 – using an exchange rate of £1 as equivalent to C$1.60). However, these prices can vary greatly, with an Arts and Humanities degree at a Canadian university ranging in price from as little as C$6,000 to as much as C$25,000. Some of the top universities in the country, such as The University of British Columbia and University of Toronto, charge the higher prices of C$20,000–25,000 for a programme in Arts and Humanities. Most universities in British Columbia, Ontario and Québec (where the majority of universities are located) would charge somewhere in the region of C$14,000–17,000 for an equivalent programme. A full list of prices is available at: www.aucc.ca/canadian-universities/facts-and-stats/tuition-fees-by-university/.

Living costs

Table 4.1 gives details of the rough costs of living in Canada.

Table 4.1 Cost of living in Canada

Cost	Price
Application fees	The cost of applying to the universities will vary, but is often around C$50. One should plan on applying to around four or five universities, so around C$250 should be budgeted for application fees.
Accommodation and living costs	Including accommodation and food, your living costs should be around C$10,000–15,000. This will depend on the choices you make regarding your accommodation, and social life. A two-bed private apartment, for example, can cost anywhere between C$500–1,000 per month, while a room in halls of residence can be between C$4,000–6,500 per year.
Books and supplies	C$1,000 is estimated as the cost of books and supplies for undergraduate courses. However, these costs may be brought down by purchasing the necessary books second hand and by making use of the library facilities.
Health insurance	Health insurance in Canada costs approximately C$600. This includes all doctor or hospital visits and is organised through your university. You will receive a health card with your own number which is valid for use anywhere in Canada.
Other living costs	Other living costs such as running a mobile phone, transportation and travel should be budgeted in. This will largely depend on where in the country you live (a student 'metropass' in Toronto will cost $93.50 per month for example). Around C$1,500 should be a conservative estimate.

Financial aid

While Canadian universities do not have the financial resources to match the scholarship offers of the larger private universities of the USA it is still possible to receive scholarships. Many universities award automatic scholarships for international students meeting certain academic entry level requirements. It is important that you contact the individual institutions you are applying to regarding financial aid, as most programmes are run by the universities themselves as opposed to being run at a national level. Note that more information on scholarships available, dependent on your country of origin, can be found at the following website: https://w01.scholarships-bourses.gc.ca/scholarshipnoncdn-boursenon cdn.aspx?lang=eng

For postgraduate students there are also a variety of independent scholarship-awarding foundations which can help with the costs of tuition and living. This is again something that the universities you are applying to will be able to advise on, although for UK students, the Trudeau Foundation, Jeanne Sauvé Youth Foundation and Canadian Government offer lucrative scholarships in the shape of the Trudeau Scholarships, Sauvé Scholars Program and Vanier Canada Graduate Scholarships which are worth researching.

Further to financial aid in the form of scholarships, there are programmes designed to allow full-time international students to work off campus while completing their studies. For more information on this please see the 'Student life in Canada' section.

Student loans

Unfortunately, international students studying on a student visa are not eligible for bank loans or government student loans in Canada. These are only possible if you have a guarantor who is a permanent resident or citizen. If you are in the process of obtaining permanent residency or have someone who is a permanent resident and is willing to be a co-signer then loan opportunities are possible.

Applying to your universities

Time frame

It is advised that you begin the application process as early as eight months before you wish to begin studying at your chosen university. You will need to go through the whole application procedure for your individual universities before being able to apply for a study permit to go and study in Canada, so it is recommended that you allow the maximum amount of time possible. Most universities announce their decisions between four and six months of the application deadlines. These deadlines will be listed on the university websites, and it is a good idea to make a list of all the deadlines for your different universities of choice before doing anything else so that you know what you are working towards.

Application procedure

Application procedures will vary from university to university and from province to province as a result of the devolved nature of the education system in Canada. You can expect to pay an application fee in the region of C$50 for most university applications. This fee is designed to deter people who are not really committed to studying at the university from sending in an application. It is recommended that you spend a lot of time carefully choosing a handful of institutions that you are interested in applying to, in order to avoid the costs becoming too great.

While less emphasis is placed on SAT (for undergraduates) and GRE (for postgraduates) examinations in Canada than it is in the USA, some universities and some programmes require international students to have taken said examinations. Some other universities, while not demanding SAT or GRE scores for admission, recommend attaching scores in these examinations for applications. Often the results of these tests will be taken into account for the awarding of scholarships, particularly at graduate level. It is advisable to consult the individual faculty website for the universities and programmes that you are interested in to see if SAT or GRE scores are required. If you are applying to Canadian universities as well as US universities, then it is recommended that you take the SAT or GRE examinations and attach your scores to all applications, as US universities will most likely require them, and Canadian universities will look favourably on students listing their scores in these tests. (For more detailed information about what the SAT and GRE examinations consist of and how they are taken, please consult the 'Standardised examinations' section of Chapter 3, USA, in this book.)

Once you have consulted individual university websites and ascertained what is needed to make an application, most university applications can be made online and many provinces and territories have centralised application systems for online applications which you will be directed to by the universities themselves. You will need to provide copies of your A Level and/or degree transcripts along with references and in some cases examples of written work. Once you have uploaded all the necessary documentation and paid the application fee, you can wait to hear back from your universities. Note that many universities require original documents to be sent to them. It is better if possible to send notarised (legalised) copies of the documents, if necessary with Foreign and Commonwealth Office Apostilles, instead. You do not want to have your original documents out of reach while applying to various universities, and you also run the risk of losing your only original copy in the post.

Visa information

Study permit

Once you have been notified of your acceptance to a Canadian university, you will need to think about obtaining a study permit. To obtain a study permit you need to complete an application form and send it to one of the following: the Canadian

Consulate in Edinburgh, Cardiff or Belfast; or the Canadian High Commission in London. You can find the necessary information on their websites. You will not normally need to have an interview to obtain your study permit, but in certain instances you may be required to. You are advised to apply at least two months before you would need your study permit. The application forms can be downloaded from the following website: www.cic.gc.ca/english/information/applications/student.asp

What is needed?

In order to obtain the study permit you need the following:

1   To have been accepted by an educational institution in Canada.
2   To be able to prove that you have the money to pay for your tuition fees, living expenses and return transportation to and from Canada.
3   To be able to prove that you are a law-abiding citizen with no criminal record. You may have to provide a police certificate.
4   To be in good health and willing to complete a medical examination if necessary, although this is not usually required of UK students.
5   To satisfy the immigration office that you will leave Canada at the end of your authorised stay.

What are the steps in applying?

The steps in applying for a study permit are the following:

1   Check the application processing time (currently eight to ten weeks).
2   Determine where you will submit your application.
3   Collect together the necessary documents.
4   Complete your application form.
5   Pay the correct processing fee (currently C$125).
6   Submit the application form and additional documentation.

What is the documentation required?

The following are the supporting documents that are usually required:

1   Original letter of acceptance from your university.
2   Proof of identity in the form of a valid passport.
3   Two photographs of yourself.
4   Proof of financial support while you study in Canada, usually in the form of your bank statements for the past four months.
5   The original letter awarding any scholarships or bursaries which you have been granted either by the university or by any external bodies.
6   A police certificate or certificate of good conduct.

Once you have been accepted you will be sent a letter by the visa office stating your approval for a study permit. This is not the permit itself but must be taken with you to Canada and shown to immigration officials at your point of entry in order to obtain your actual study permit. You should also carry your letter of acceptance from your university with you at this time.

CAQ (Québec)

Those applying to study in Québec will have to obtain a CAQ from the Gouvernement du Québec *as well* as their study permit from the Canadian Government. This takes an extra 20 business days to issue, and so those applying to university in Québec should allow a greater amount of time to the total scheduled for visa applications. For further information regarding the process of obtaining a CAQ please consult the following website: www.immigration-quebec. gouv.qc.ca/en/index.html

What is needed?

1 Payment of the application fee (currently C$104).
2 Acceptance by a Québécois educational institution.
3 Agreement to the conditions of the CAQ:
   a Making your studies your primary activity in Québec.
   b Maintaining your own health and hospitalisation insurance plan.
4 Possessing sufficient funds for:
   a Tuition fees.
   b Return flights.
   c Settling expenses in Québec (C$500).
   d Living expenses (calculated as C$11,557 per year in 2012).
   e Cost of health and hospitalisation insurance.

Student life in Canada

Campus life

Campus life in Canada is comparable to that in the USA, with a big emphasis on societies and sports. As in the USA, fraternities and sororities are a big part of campus life, and for information regarding this please see the 'Campus life' section of Chapter 3, USA, in this book. At Canadian universities you will find a vast array of societies and activities you can take part in. Engaging in social and sports activities is a good way to make contact with other students outside of those doing your course or those who you live with. It is also a good way to make friends with Canadian students. In Canada, the national sports are ice hockey and lacrosse, although you will find plenty of opportunities to take part in a wide range of sports.

Canadian campuses are very safe, and most run patrol cars and have 24-hour security to ensure the safety of students. There is also usually a Campus Security Office which can be contacted at any time. One key difference between the USA and Canada is that while the legal drinking age is 21 in the USA, in Canada it is either 18 or 19, depending on the territory or province. This means that for undergraduates, UK students can expect a university nightlife a little more comparable to what they would experience back in the UK. Those studying in cities and towns near to the US border will find that many American undergraduate students cross the border to go for nights out, creating a thriving nightlife. Note that the legal drinking age is 18 in Québec, Manitoba and Alberta. The legal drinking age is 19 in all other provinces and territories.

It is important to remember that while the university campus and campus bars are very secure, when going outside of the university it is important to be careful. Canada is a very safe country by and large, but it is still important to take precautions, especially while you are acclimatising. Taxis in both Canada and the USA are considerably cheaper than they are in the UK, and as a result are an affordable and safe way of travelling around, especially at night.

Accommodation and student living

In terms of accommodation in Canada, most students prefer dormitories which are the Canadian equivalent of halls of residence, where you will share kitchen, laundry and bathroom facilities with other students. Dormitories can be a good option as they are usually located near to the university campus and mean that you are in regular contact with fellow students. This can be particularly helpful at first, when you are dealing with living away from friends and family for the first time. Having a bunch of students around who are in the same position as you can be a real plus. Although they can be a good option, dormitories can be relatively expensive, and it is advisable to investigate prices before committing as some residence fees in Canada can be upwards of C$8,000 per year.

You may thus choose to live in dormitories for your first year, or even just the first semester, while you acclimatise and give yourself time to search for private accommodation. When searching for private accommodation it is a good idea to contact the housing office or student's union at the university or college at which you study, as they often provide information about accommodation local to the campus. Rent prices can vary greatly from city to city and also depending on the type of accommodation you are seeking. Thus estimates can range from as little as C$400 to C$1,500 per month.

Factors which will affect your price will be whether you choose to share with other students, what quality of accommodation you are looking for and where you are located. As a general example, Toronto and Vancouver are recognised as being the most expensive cities in Canada, and thus you can expect to pay more in these cities than in others. When paying rent, always ask for a receipt as proof of payment to avoid any legal difficulties.

Healthcare

In terms of healthcare, each province or territory is in charge of its own healthcare system. Almost all universities and colleges have healthcare plans for their international students, so the best thing to do is contact the university or college you are applying to and ask them directly about the specifics of any healthcare plan they offer (i.e. what it covers and what it costs). Evidence of having a healthcare plan will be necessary to be able to study in Canada, and costs are often estimated at around C$600.

Work while you study

In the first instance, university and college students are able to work on campus without any sort of work permit. The possibility of working on campus is largely dependent on the size of your institution and usually involves something like library work for example. The larger the university you study at the larger the number and size of the various on-campus facilities will be, and thus the more openings there will be for students to work on campus.

However, it is also possible for international students to work off campus, as long as they are registered at a university or college participating in the Off-Campus Work Permit Program. Eligible students will be able to work up to 20 hours per week during term time, and full-time during all study breaks. This is a very useful way for international students to subsidise their studies and support themselves while in Canada. Eligibility to participate in the Program is dependent upon:

1   The student possessing a valid study permit.
2   The student having been enrolled for at least six months prior to applying for the Program at an eligible post-secondary institution.
3   The institution at which the student is enrolled having signed an agreement with the province or territory with which they participate. This agreement will involve monitoring and reporting on the student's academic record in order to maintain the student's continued eligibility.

This means that in order to participate in the Program you have to wait until you are six months into your degree, and must not let your academic record slip while working. The university or college you are studying at will be responsible for monitoring your progress.

Further practical information

Transport

If you plan on running a car while studying in Canada, then you are advised to apply for an International Driver's Permit (IDP). In order to obtain an IDP you must have a valid driver's licence in the UK. In Canada, the only authorised authority to issue you with an IDP is the Canadian Automobile Association (CAA), for a fee of C$15. The IDP is valid for one year at a time, and you must renew your IDP for each year you plan to run your car in Canada.

Although gasoline is much cheaper in Canada than it is in the UK (at the time of writing a gallon of gasoline costs US$4.76 in Canada compared to US$8.06 in the UK), running a car can be expensive, and if you think that the university or college you are applying to would require you to run a car then you should factor this into your budget.

If you are living in a big city, then you should also consider the cost of public transport. Most cities have student discounts on monthly transport passes. The price can vary greatly from city to city: in Toronto a monthly student transport pass currently costs C$93.50, compared to Vancouver (C$30), Montréal (C$43.75), Calgary (C$94.00), Ottawa (C$76.75), Edmonton (C$84.65).

Banking

Banks in Canada usually charge for using their services, and maintaining a bank account at a Canadian bank costs about C$5 per month, but often offer individualised student accounts to meet your needs. The major banks in Canada are the Royal Bank of Canada, Scotia Bank, HSBC Canada, Bank of Montréal, President's Choice Bank and the Canadian Imperial Bank of Commerce.

Mobile phones

In Canada, as in the USA, mobile phones are called cell phones. When moving to Canada one of the first things you will want to do is set up a cell phone contract. Monthly plans in Canada start at about C$20, and this is a necessary expense to include in your budget.

Climate

Temperatures in Canada during the winter period can be extreme – this is perhaps the biggest difference from the UK in terms of climate. Investing in winter clothing in Canada is a necessary expenditure, and preparing yourself for cold Canadian winters is very important. You can expect to spend between C$250–500 on winter clothing.

Restaurant etiquette

Like in the USA, tipping is the accepted norm in restaurants, with somewhere around 15–20 per cent being an advisable amount to tip. Furthermore, when shopping in Canada in general, you must remember that sales tax is not included on the prices of items. You must bear in mind that a 5–15 per cent (depending on the territory or province) tax is going to be added on to the price shown.

After you finish your degree

One of the major benefits of studying at a Canadian university is that you are easily able to apply for permanent residence in Canada. There is a direct route offered to international graduates of Canadian universities called the 'Canadian Experience Class'. The minimum requirements are that:

1   The graduate is planning on living outside of Québec.
2   The graduate has at least one year of full-time experience of skilled work in Canada.
3   The one year of full-time experience should be gained legally, i.e. with the relevant authorisation on either a work or study visa.
4   The graduate has applied within a year of said work experience.

In order to get the necessary work experience to apply for permanent residence in Canada there is a Post-Graduate Work Permit Program (PGWPP) which allows international graduates of Canadian universities to stay and work in Canada for a determined period of time. This will allow you to accrue the necessary one year of full-time skilled work in Canada to apply for the 'Canadian Experience Class' permanent residency programme.

For more information you can consult Citizenship and Immigration Canada, and their helpful section on the 'PGWPP' and 'Canadian Experience Class' applications at the following website: www.cic.gc.ca/english/immigrate/cec/index.asp

As an international graduate of a Canadian university you are thus able to open up another labour market for yourself. Whether you choose to stay and work in Canada permanently, or pick up the years' experience through the PGWPP before looking back to the UK or elsewhere for permanent full-time employment, being a graduate of a Canadian university offers you great possibilities.

If you do choose to return to the UK, your Canadian degree will set you apart from other UK students, and Canadian qualifications are among the most highly rated at an international level. So look forward to a bright future in the workplace, after having had the unique experience of a university life in one of the most beautiful countries on earth.

Chapter 5

Australia

Orientation

Introduction

Australia is the sixth largest country in the world, and is one of the world's largest island nations. The country has three time zones; the Eastern time zone (GMT +10), the Central time zone (GMT +9.5) and the Western time zone (GMT +8). However, despite its large size, the country has a relatively small population

compared to the UK, totalling just 22 million. Similar to Canada, this is down to the extreme living conditions across much of the centre of the country, with the population concentrated around the coastal areas. The most populous cities in Australia are Sydney (New South Wales) 4,667,283; Melbourne (Victoria) 2,246,345; Brisbane (Queensland) 2,189,878; Perth (Western Australia) 1,897,548; and Adelaide (South Australia) 1,227,174. The majority of the population live on the Eastern and South-Eastern coast. For this reason, many of the higher education establishments are to be found in this part of the country.

Despite its smaller population, according to the IMF rankings for 2012, Australia has the 12th largest economy in the world. This relative economic prosperity, coupled with a variety of other factors, led to the country being rated as the second best place to live in the world in a study carried out by the United Nations. It is no wonder then that over the last few years Australia has become a very popular destination for many immigrants as well as a top destination for international students.

Reasons to study in Australia

- Australia is ranked by the United Nations as the second best place to live in the world.
- Australia is a politically stable, multicultural and safe country to study in.
- Tuition fees in Australia are comparable to those paid by international students in the USA, Canada and the UK.
- International students can work up to 20 hours per week during term time, and unlimited hours during holidays, to subsidise their living costs while studying.
- There is a streamlined visa application procedure for graduates of Australian universities wishing to continue working in the country upon graduation from their degree.
- Higher education in Australia is recognised for its quality the world over, making graduates with Australian qualifications competitive on the international market.

Higher education in Australia

Finding your course and institution

Each year around 180,000 students choose to enrol on higher education programmes in Australia. While many of these students are either Chinese (40 per cent) or Malaysian (7.2 per cent) there are increasing numbers of students from all around the world who come to study in Australia. In 2012, there were 1,186 UK students enrolled on higher education programmes in the country (data taken from the Australian Government's 'Australian Education International' website, https://aei.gov.au/research/International-Student-Data/Pages/default.aspx)ʼ making it the third main non-European destination for UK students.

The higher education sector in Australia has grown hugely from the start of the millennium, and is now Australia's second largest export. There are currently 38 public and four private universities in Australia offering a wide variety of undergraduate and postgraduate programmes in a number of different fields. Australian universities are self-accrediting institutions, usually having their own legislation which often mirrors that of the state or territory. This means that there is often great variation between different programmes at different universities, so you would be wise to look into the specifics of what is offered and what is required of you at each university for the programme of your choice.

Despite this relative autonomy, as a rule of thumb Bachelor's degrees in Australia take three years to complete, like in the UK, although some professional programmes such as Law may last four years, with other programmes such as Medicine and Dentistry lasting even longer. Three-year programmes may be extended to four years whereby students will be awarded a BA (Hons) rather than a BA. Master's degrees in Australia are usually one and a half to two years in length, but depend on the institution. The academic year in Australia is also usually divided into two semesters (although Bond University has three trimesters). The first semester will typically begin in February and finish in June for the winter break. (Remember that the seasons in Australia are the inverse of those in the UK, with winter occurring in the months of June/July.) The second semester then begins in July, with a summer break lasting from December to the following February. Students are often able to enrol on to either of these semesters, but again this depends on the institution.

When you begin your search for the ideal programme and institution in Australia a useful starting place to refine your search is by using the 'Advanced Search' feature on the following website: http://studyinaustralia.gov.au/Courses. Here you can search through the different universities by programme and location, which will most likely be two of the most important criteria when looking for a programme. You can then further narrow down your results depending on other factors which might be important to you, such as whether you would like to study at a campus university, or in a big city. It is useful to make a list of the different factors which are important to you which you can then use as a checklist when going through the results to find which programme is ideally suited to you.

It is also important to note that Australian universities are required by law to be registered with the Australian Government, so make sure to check that the university which interests you is in the list of legitimate establishments, which is the 'Commonwealth Register of Institutions and Courses for Overseas Students (CRICOS)' available at the following website: www.cricos.deewr.gov.au.

Group of 8: The Australian equivalent of the Russell Group (UK) or Ivy League (USA) is the 'Group of 8' or 'G8'. The group was formed in 1994 and is based on a focus on research quality and a comprehensive offer of general and pro-fessional education. The establishments included within the G8 are: University of

Western Australia, Australian National University, The University of Sydney, The University of Melbourne, The University of Queensland, Monash University, The University of New South Wales, The University of Adelaide.

Note: While university rankings are by no means the be-all-and-end-all of your search for the perfect university course, it may be worthwhile considering that according to the Times Higher Education World University Rankings (2012–13) six Australian universities are ranked in the top 100: University of Melbourne (28), Australian National University (37), University of Sydney (62), University of Queensland (65), University of New South Wales (85) and Monash University (99).

The credit system

There is no universal credit system across the different universities of Australia, and each programme has its own points system. A typical credit load for one semester at a university could be anything from 12 to 50 points. However, all universities do implement a credit system whereby each module or course is assigned a certain number of credits. Students will then have to complete a certain number of credits across their programme in order to graduate. Although the different crediting systems are expressed in different numerical values, students should remember that they will correspond to a similar workload overall across all Australian universities.

Note: For the purposes of transferring across different universities, Australian universities do recognise the ECTS (European Credit Transfer System) and are by and large good at recognising the value of credits assigned at different universities within Australia.

The grading of your final diploma in Australia is usually expressed in the following way:

Higher Distinction (HD) – *Usually anything above 80 or 85 per cent*
Distinction (D) – *Usually anything above 70 or 75 per cent*
Credit (C) – *Usually anything above 60 or 65 per cent*
Pass (P) – *Always above 50 per cent*
Fail (N) – *Always below 50 per cent*

However, there are some exceptions to this method of awarding results. Melbourne University, for example, grades its students in the same way that UK universities do (1st, 2:1, 2:2, 3rd or Fail), while La Trope and University of Southern Queensland offer grades in the form of A, B, C and D.

Furthermore, GPAs are also sometimes referred to in Australia (although never below university level). The formula is more complicated than in other countries and can be expressed in the following way: *GPA = Sum of (grade points x course unit value) / total number of credits attempted.* Students should not worry too much about their GPA unless their university frequently refers to it, as GPAs are used more hermetically in Australia than in the USA or Canada.

Given the lack of uniformity in crediting systems and in the awarding of degrees, it is important that students familiarise themselves with the system of the university they have chosen to study at. It will be important for students to know, for example, how many credits each course is worth and how many credits they need to graduate. This is because only then will they be able to calculate how many courses they need to take per semester to graduate on time. It will furthermore be of use to them to know whether they need 70 or 75 per cent to earn a Distinction if this is the result that they are aiming for.

Financing your studies

Tuition fees and living costs

Tuition fees

In Australia, tuition fees vary from university to university and from programme to programme. The variety is huge, and for an undergraduate programme the tuition can vary between 14,000 AUD and 35,000 AUD (AUD stands for Australian Dollar and at the time of writing £1 is equal to roughly 1.5 AUD). This is equivalent to £9,100 and £22,900 respectively.

Australia is thus not a cheap option for UK students, and this is increasingly the case as time goes on, as the AUD is becoming more and more competitive with the Pound over time, making studying in Australia more and more expensive for UK students. However, the prices at the moment are still comparable with those paid by international students for equivalent degrees at American, British and Canadian universities.

Students will often find that tuition is calculated at a 'cost per unit' basis, rather than a yearly rate such as is charged in the UK. What this means is that each course or unit which is available at the university, as well as having its own individual credit value, also has its own monetary value. As the degree will have a minimum number of credits needed, students can thus work out how much their degree is likely to cost by working out the average price of the courses, and then multiplying it by the number of courses they will need to take per year. For example: four courses per semester at an average price of 2,500 AUD will cost roughly 10,000 AUD per semester. Thus, eight courses per year at the average price of 2,500 AUD will cost roughly 20,000 AUD per year. For this reason you will often find that the tuition fee listed 'per year' is often asterisked explaining that this is only a rough estimate, as some courses may cost more than others, and the exact tuition fee per year will depend on which courses a student chooses to take.

It is thus very important that students consult university websites in order to find information about a) how many courses (or units) you are required to take each year, and b) a list of the prices of each of the courses (or units). Only then can students make an educated evaluation of whether or not they will be able to afford the programme of their choice.

Living costs

Aside from tuition fees, you need to consider the price of living in Australia while pursuing your studies. Some preliminary information can be found in the Table 5.1, however, in general students should expect a similar cost of living to that which they would experience in the UK.

Table 5.1 Cost of living in Australia

Cost	Price
Application fees	Most Australian universities charge between 50–100 AUD. One should apply to around three or four universities, so around 200 AUD should be budgeted for application fees.
Accommodation	Accommodation, including bills, should cost between 7,000–15,000 AUD. This will depend on whether students live on campus (and have meals included) or in private accommodation. Private accommodation will also vary in price depending on a number of factors. For more detailed information about accommodation, as well as other information about living in Australia, please consult the 'Student life in Australia' section.
Living costs	For those living on campus, the higher price of accommodation is often offset by having your meals provided for you. Otherwise a monthly food bill will be around 500 AUD. The amount set for living costs for an academic year is 18,610 AUD and is required to be available as funds for students to apply for a visa.
Books and supplies	The cost of textbooks and other supplies can be around 1,000 AUD in total for an undergraduate course, although this can be brought down by purchasing second hand and making use of library facilities.
Health	The average cost of a minimum 'Overseas Student Health Cover' is around 437 AUD per year, but this will depend on which provider you choose and the extent of the health cover you opt for.
Other costs	Other costs will include running a mobile phone, social expenses and transport costs, all of which will be dependent on where you live in the country. A conservative estimate of 1,500 AUD per year should be given.

Financial aid

There is not as much funding available through universities in Australia as there is in other countries such as in the USA. However, students are still advised to consult the websites of each of the individual universities they are interested in applying to as they do sometimes run scholarships for international students. There are merit-based scholarships for both undergraduate and postgraduate students at University of Sydney, Macquarie University, University of Melbourne, University of Adelaide and La Trobe, while at University of Newcastle, University of Western Australia and Flinders University merit-based scholarships are also available but only at postgraduate level.

There are many scholarships offered through the Australian Government or ancillary organisations, but many of these are targeted specifically at citizens of developing countries and are not available to UK students. However, postgraduate research students would be advised to look into the International Postgraduate Research Scholarships (IPRS), of which 330 are awarded each year, or the Endeavour Postgraduate Scholarship Awards.

For information about the scholarships which might be available to you it is advised you consult the following website: www.studyinaustralia.gov.au/Scholarships.

Student loans

Unfortunately international students are not eligible to apply for student loans. However, some universities do offer loans for international students (though usually not in their first or final year) for part of the tuition fees, but these usually require an Australian citizen as a guarantor.

Students with Australian citizenship should look into the HECS-HELP loan offered by the Australian Government to domestic students.

Applying to your universities

Time frame

Students will find that they can often apply for entry to either of the two semesters. It is thus important for students to begin researching the different points of entry and application processes for the different universities and programmes which interest them. As a general rule of thumb, application deadlines tend to be two or three months before the entry date being applied for, but again this will vary from university to university. However, it is advised that students begin the application process long before this. Furthermore, students should factor in a three-week wait, or longer, to complete the visa application process.

Application procedure

The application procedure for Australian universities is made simpler by the fact that they do not require applicants to have SAT or GRE qualifications like their American counterparts. Australian universities will also be familiar with A Level and IB qualifications. Note that IB students are able to apply through UAC International, who work with a selection of Australian universities handling online applications for a fee: http://uac.edu.au/international/apply/who-can-appl.shtml/.

UK students will often have to have copies of their qualifications certified (to avoid working with original documents). To do this, students will need to have a Notary Public in the UK certify their documents. The student will be charged for this service and this cost should be factored into the application procedure. Please also note that in the UK, A Level certificates are often issued in November, meaning that students are unable to apply for the semester directly after their A Levels end. If you were intending on applying for a programme to start directly after the summer break following your A Level exams then you should contact the university to explain your situation.

Aside from presenting your academic documents, students will be required to fill out an application form and present other documents such as a CV. Australian universities often charge an application fee which is usually between 50–100 AUD. This fee will need to be paid in order for the application to be processed, and the payment is usually taken online. While some universities have fully integrated online application systems, some will still require international students to submit applications by post. You are advised to find out if this is the case for the universities you are interested in applying to as you will then have to factor in the time it takes for the application to arrive in Australia.

Visa information

Student visa

Applying for a student visa has become much more easy and streamlined due to implementations to student visa applications which came through in 2010 after the Knight Review. Currently the process takes upwards of three weeks to complete, and should begin once the student is in possession of a Confirmation of Enrolment (COE) from an Australian university.

Further to the COE, students will also need to show evidence of Overseas Student Health Cover (see the 'Healthcare' subsection in 'Student life in Australia') and proof that you have enough money to pay for: a) travel to and from Australia; b) tuition fees; and c) living costs, which for one student are currently valued at 18,610 AUD per year.

The application can be made online, and you can apply anytime from 93 days before your course begins. Applications made before this time will be subject to a higher level of scrutiny. Family members are also able to apply as a dependent upon the same online application in order to come with you. Once the application has been submitted you will be assessed against a low assessment level (because you are a student) by the Department of Immigration and Citizenship. They will perform checks concerning your health, character and financial situation before accepting applicants and issuing a student visa. It is warned that the process can take longer than the estimated three weeks during peak periods.

In order to apply for the student visa you must submit:

1   your Confirmation of Enrolment (COE)
2   the visa application charge (535 AUD)
3   certified copies of passport
4   four recent passport-sized photographs with your name printed on the back
5   certified copies of birth certificate
6   evidence of Overseas Student Health Cover (OSHC)
7   financial documents showing you have the necessary money
8   a completed 157A application form.

The visa will allow you to study in Australia for the defined period of time, and bring any eligible dependent family members with you. You are also able to work up to 40 hours per fortnight during term time (see the 'Work while you study' subsection in 'Student life in Australia'), and unlimited hours outside of term time on the student visa. Any family members are also able to work up to 40 hours per fortnight. The student, in exchange, is required to remain enrolled on the course, to keep up attendance and to make 'satisfactory progress' on the course of study. The terms under which 'satisfactory progress' are understood is up to the institution you are studying at.

Student life in Australia

Campus life

While studying at an Australian university you should find you have a buzzing and fulfilling campus life, with most universities having a wide array of clubs and associations you can join. Australia as a country is very sport oriented, with sports such as Australian rules football, cricket, rugby and hockey being very popular. Soccer is also becoming increasingly popular down under, as the A-League becomes more competitive attracting more big name players from Europe. Most mainstream sports will be represented by at least one team you can join at a university level. Australian social life is often based around not only these team sports, but also individual disciplines such as swimming and surfing, both of which are very popular with Australians.

Unlike in the USA and Canada, university fraternities and sororities do not exist in Australia, with students instead grouping together in various associations and clubs for shared interests, either sporting or otherwise.

Students should expect a university social life which is more similar to that in the UK than one would expect to find in the USA, for example. The legal drinking age in Australia, like in the UK, is 18, and most campuses and cities will have an array of bars and nightclubs for students to attend. Campuses tend to be very safe places, with 24-hour security, and in general, as a country, Australia is a safe place. However, as would be advisable to anyone moving to a new country, students should be careful when going off campus, especially at night.

Accommodation and student living

Most Australian universities offer international students the chance to stay in university or campus accommodation. This can often be more economical for students, particularly as these student residences often provide meals for the students who are staying there. Choosing to live in university accommodation is a safe and easy option for students who are moving out to Australia as you can mix with other Australian and international students who are in your position, and have everything you need nearby for the transition period while you get used to living in a new country.

Students may choose to opt for private accommodation, however, or indeed they may move into private accommodation after having lived in university accommodation for an initial period upon arrival. There are a few choices open to students who do not want to live in university accommodation. You may choose to rent a private house or apartment in the town or city where the university is based, either sharing with other students or renting on your own. The cost of this will obviously depend on various factors, such as the quality of accommodation, whether you are sharing with other students or not and the location of the apartment. The location will affect the cost both in terms of where in the city or town the property you are renting is, but also where in the country you are studying, as some areas of the country are more expensive than others. Sydney, Melbourne and Perth, for example, are renowned for being the three most expensive cities in Australia.

The option of private accommodation could be appealing to students because of the independence it affords them. However, rental accommodation is limited and as a result is notoriously expensive. Trying to find oneself affordable rental accommodation can thus often be a headache for students, especially if you are trying to organise this for yourself from outside of Australia. Students should contact the housing or accommodation department at their university for help.

Alternatively, they may choose to go down the path of homestay, which involves lodging with a family. This option is taken up by many international students, as it gives them the support of a home life upon arrival and also includes amenities such as laundry, breakfast and dinner. It can also be a less expensive way of living outside of university accommodation. Students who are interested in this offer should look into the different agencies which help students find homestay options. University housing or accommodation departments might also have information about homestay options for international students, and it is worth contacting them to find out.

Healthcare

There is a National Healthcare system in Australia but it is a little different to the NHS in the UK. In any case, international students are required to take out health insurance; indeed it is legally required of students in order to be given a student visa. Students do not have the option to take out their own choice of health insurance abroad, but instead need to take out Overseas Student Health Cover (OSHC). It must be taken out to cover the whole period of study, and if this study period is elongated, then the health insurance must be extended.

OSHC is offered by the following insurers in Australia:

- Australian Health Management (www.ahm.com.au/oshc/oshc)
- UPA Australia (www.bupa.com.au/health-insurance/cover/oshc)
- Medibank Private (www.medibank.com.au/Client/StaticPages/OSHC Home.aspx)
- Allianz Global Assistance (https://oshcallianzassistance.com.au)
- nib OSHC (www.nib.com.au/home/newtonib/overseasstudents/ Pages/overseasstudents.aspx)

You can purchase OSHC through any of the above websites or indirectly through the education provider where you are going to study your programme. There are different levels of cover which you should read through carefully. The average price of minimum cover is 437 AUD per year and will include:

- 100 per cent of in-patient medical services such as surgery.
- Out-of-hospital services such as visiting a GP, up to the amount specified.
- Public and, in some cases, private hospital accommodation.
- Day surgery accommodation.
- Some prosthetic devices.
- Ambulance services.
- Pharmaceuticals, up to a certain amount specified.

In the case of emergency treatment, or visiting a GP, you will not need to contact your OSHC provider; however, for non-emergency trips to hospital or for private healthcare, students should contact their provider first to make sure they are covered. When you then receive your bills you will have the choice of paying it yourself and then retroactively claiming back from your provider, or directly presenting the bill to your provider for them to pay.

Work while you study

Students have the right to work on their student visa. Employers are able to check your eligibility to work by checking your visa situation online, as your details are kept electronically by the Australian Government once you are accepted for a student visa. The system they have to access is called VEVO (Visa Entitlement Verification Online) and can be checked at the following website: www.immi.gov.au/e_visa/vevo.html/

Students are only able to begin work once they have begun their course of studies, and are able to work up to 40 hours per fortnight during term time. Outside of term time students are able to work unlimited hours on their student visa. Charity work and work which is included as part of your course of study are not counted in the 40 fortnightly hours.

Further practical information

Transport

If students plan on using public transport regularly, then they would be advised to look into monthly passes, which are often discounted for students. A monthly transport pass in most major Australian cities usually costs between 100–150 AUD per month.

If you plan on running a car in Australia, there are several things to note. First, students are urged to be very cautious when purchasing second hand cars as there are many unreliable vehicles for sale on the Australian market. It is advised that students have the vehicle checked first by a qualified mechanic. Once you have purchased a vehicle it is important that you register the vehicle with the state government, or transfer the existent registration into your name. In order to be able to do this you will have to purchase Compulsory Third Party (CTP) Insurance. This is non-negotiable for running a car in Australia. You should check out the costs of running a car to make sure it is economical before committing to the purchase. Note a gallon of gasoline costs US$6.31 in Australia according to the Bloomberg Gas Price Ranking 2013, compared to US$8.06 in the UK.

Banking

By and large it is free to open a bank account in Australia, and it is relatively simple to do so. You will simply need to take your passport down to the bank when you want to set one up.

Mobile phones

The main mobile phone providers in Australia are Telstra, Optus, Vodafone and 3. It might be advisable for students to use pre-paid SIM cards in order to avoid getting locked in to any long-term contracts if you do not intend to stay in the country after graduation.

Seasons

It is important for students to remember that the seasons are the diametric opposite of those in the UK. Thus if you are starting your programme in July, you should prepare to be flying out into the Australian winter and remember to pack accordingly!

After you finish your degree

Australian higher education is internationally recognised for its quality, and students graduating with Australian undergraduate or postgraduate qualifications will find themselves being very competitive on the international job market.

Although students do not automatically have the right to stay in Australia once they finish their degree, there are a variety of different skilled worker visas which international graduates can apply for. The most common type is the 485 Skilled Graduate Temporary visa, which allows graduates to remain in the country for up to 18 months to get some work experience upon the completion of their degree.

This visa has two streams: one is the Graduate Work Stream which is available to students who have completed at least two years of study in a subject which relates to occupations on the Skilled Occupation List (SOL). The SOL can be found at the following website: http://immi.gov.au/skilled/_pdf/sol-schedule1. pdf. The other stream is called the Post Study Work Stream, whereby students must have completed a course which is registered on the Commonwealth Register for Institutions and Courses for Overseas Students (CRICOS). CRICOS can be found at the following website: http://cricos.deewr.gov.au/. The drawback to the 485 Skilled Graduate Temporary visa is the application cost, which currently stands at 1,250 AUD.

Other visa options for students wishing to stay on in Australia are:

- 402 Training and Research visa
- 487 Regional Sponsored visa
- 887 Skilled Regional Residence visa
- 885 Skilled Independent Residence visa
- 886 Skilled Sponsor Residence visa

These different visa options will allow you to remain in Australia for different amounts of time and have different application criteria, some requiring sponsorship by a company or employer. In order to find out about visa options once you graduate it is best to visit your university counsellor once you are already studying in Australia.

Whether you end up staying on to work in Australia, or whether you choose to return to work in the UK or indeed elsewhere abroad, you will find that an Australian higher education will prepare you well for the international job market and will also prove to be an unforgettable experience.

Chapter 6

New Zealand

Orientation

Introduction

New Zealand is a Pacific island nation which is comprised of two main islands called North Island and South Island. New Zealand is similar in size to the UK, but its population is considerably smaller, with only 4.4 million New Zealanders inhabiting the islands. Of these 4.4 million, the vast majority live on the North Island where the most populous cities are, with only 1 million people living on the South Island. Despite this, the eight universities in New Zealand are fairly evenly spread between the two islands, with three universities having campuses on the South Island.

New Zealand is known for its stunning scenery and high standard of living. It was ranked as the 6th best place to live in 2013 by the United Nations Human Development Index. The largest cities in New Zealand are Auckland (1,397,000), Wellington (395,000), Christchurch (375,000) and Hamilton (209,300).

Reasons to study in New Zealand

- New Zealand is ranked by the United Nations as one of the best places to live in the world.
- New Zealand is the third safest country in the world according to the 2013 Global Peace Index, making it an ideal place to study and live.
- Tuition fees in New Zealand are comparable to those charged by universities in the UK, the USA and Australia for international students.
- New Zealand is world renowned for its natural beauty.
- The quality of education in New Zealand is recognised worldwide.

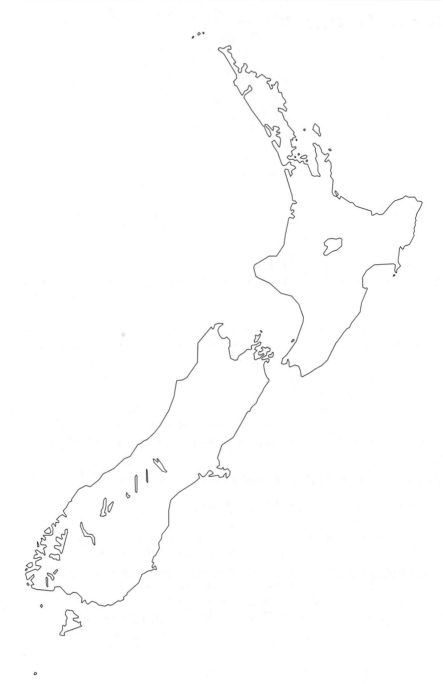

Higher education in New Zealand

Finding your course and institution

The higher education, or tertiary education, sector in New Zealand is relatively small when compared to countries such as the USA, Australia and Canada. However, this can be put down to the much smaller population and there are still 18,300 students enrolled on higher education programmes in New Zealand. Of these, the majority come from China, but a number of UK students choose to study in New Zealand every year.

> Language note: As in Australia, higher education is often called 'tertiary education' in New Zealand.

Bachelor's degrees in New Zealand will typically last three years. However, students are usually able to do one extra year at the end of the Bachelor's degree which will convert this into an Honours degree or BA (Hons). Master's degrees in New Zealand typically last two years for international students, although for those who have completed the four-year BA (Hons) degree this can be reduced to just one year.

There are eight universities in New Zealand, all of which are public. These are the following:

- Auckland University of Technology
- Massey University
- University of Auckland
- University of Waikato
- Victoria University of Wellington
- University of Canterbury
- University of Otago
- Lincoln University

Of these universities, the last three are located on the South Island, while the first five are located on the North Island. It is worth noting that some of these universities have multiple campuses, some in different cities, thus students should check which campus the programme they are interested in is run at. All of the universities offer a range of subjects in both the arts and sciences. All universities in New Zealand work on a two-semester calendar similar to that used by most Australian universities. Semester 1 will typically begin in February and run through until June. Semester 2 will typically begin in July and run through until November.

The limited number of universities in New Zealand means that students should be able to look through the relevant programmes run at each university in order to ascertain which ones might be of interest to them. They may also want to consider the location of the university, and a number of other factors. At the following website students can look through a brochure of the universities in New Zealand which might help them narrow down their interests: www.universitiesnz. ac.nz/files/2013%20NZ%20Universities%20Directory.pdf/.

Note: While university rankings are by no means the be-all-and-end-all of your search for the ideal university course, it may be worthwhile considering that the only New Zealand University in the QS World University Rankings is University of Auckland, which is also the highest ranking New Zealand university in the Times Higher Education World University Rankings.

The credit system

The credit system in New Zealand is based on 120 credits being the typical credit load for one academic year. Each programme is then given its own value in credits, and students will need to take enough courses over the duration of their degree to complete the 360 required credits (for a three-year undergraduate degree), or the 480 required credits (for a four-year BA (Hons) degree). One credit is supposed to be valued at ten notional learning hours.

Degrees in New Zealand are awarded in the same classifications that they are in the UK (1st, 2:1, 2:2, 3rd or Fail).

Financing your studies

Tuition fees and living costs

Tuition fees

In New Zealand for undergraduate courses, tuition fees are usually charged at anywhere between 20,000 NZ$ and 30,000 NZ$, which is roughly equivalent to £10,500 and £16,000. This will of course depend on the course and on the particular university, however. The tuition fee for postgraduate courses is usually similar, or fractionally higher, than that for undergraduate courses. Certain courses, such as Medicine, Veterinary Medicine and Dentistry can be very expensive for students, with the latter sometimes costing as much as 80,000 NZ$ (£42,800) per year. Note that at the time of writing, £1 is equal to 1.85 NZ$.

Living costs

Aside from tuition fees, you need to consider the price of living in New Zealand while pursuing your studies. Please consult Table 6.1 for more information.

Table 6.1 Cost of living in New Zealand

Cost	Price
Application fees	Most universities in New Zealand do not charge application fees.
Accommodation	Accommodation in New Zealand should cost between 9,000–15,000 NZ$. This will depend on whether students live on campus (and have meals included) or choose to rent private accommodation. The price of private accommodation will also depend on a variety of factors. For more information about accommodation please see the 'Student life in New Zealand' section.
Living costs	Living costs will be variable, but most universities estimate between 12,000–20,000 NZ$ per academic year. International students are required to have a minimum of 15,000 NZ$ per year for living costs when applying for a visa.
Books and supplies	Between 500–1,000 NZ$ should be budgeted for the costs of books and stationary during your degree.
Health	A yearly health plan with StudentSafe costs 585 NZ$.
Other costs	Other costs will include running a mobile phone, social expenses and transport costs, all of which will depend on where you live in the country. A conservative estimate of 1,500 NZ$ should be given per year.

Financial aid

Unfortunately there are not many opportunities for funding for international students wishing to study in New Zealand, particularly at undergraduate level. Students are still advised, however, to contact the subject departments or International Office of the universities they are applying to asking about any opportunities for funding, as New Zealand universities themselves do occasionally offer limited funding to students.

Postgraduate applicants are advised to look into the Commonwealth Scholarships and Fellowships Plan which offer scholarships and funding for Master's degree and PhD programmes. UK students should consult the following website which offers funding for PhD students in New Zealand: http://cscuk. dfid.gov.uk/apply/scholarships-uk-citizens/new-zealand/

Applying to your universities

Time frame

Application deadlines are usually at the beginning of May (for Semester 1) and of December (for Semester 2). However, students should begin the application process much earlier, as they are likely to need to have certain documents legalised in the UK, and in some cases to send in applications by post; both of which can take time and should be accounted for. Up to five months should be allowed in order for students to properly research their different options and then submit full applications to the universities of their choice.

Application procedure

The application procedure may differ from university to university, and students are advised to carefully read the relevant section of each potential university's website to make sure they are familiar with what is required of them. In general, for undergraduate programmes, New Zealand universities require students to submit a completed application form (unique to each university), certified copies of school leaving certificates and certified copies of their passports.

Universities in New Zealand require the certified copies in order to ascertain whether the qualifications are authentic or not. This process can be undertaken with any Notary Public. Students should thus factor the cost of certifying their documents into the cost of the application.

As students need to have their school leaving certificate (e.g. A Levels or IB) certified in order to make an application, students may have trouble meeting the deadline for application in early December, as A Level certificates are released in November. Students in this position should contact the university explaining their position, and often universities will have systems in place to get around this. Note that some universities may allow students to send certified copies of their AS Levels, for example, while their A Level certificates are being procured. If not, students wishing to study in New Zealand may have to take a gap year between their A Levels and their degree which would start in July of the following year.

Postgraduate applications follow a similar pattern, but will require students to provide additional documentation, which might include a CV, a research proposal, letters of recommendation and certified copies of their university transcripts. Application deadlines for postgraduate students may differ from those for undergraduates and students should consult each university's website individually. Postgraduate students may also find that they may be obliged to begin their programme in Semester 1.

Visa information

Student visa

Students can only apply for a student visa once they have been offered a place at a New Zealand university, and have Confirmation of Enrolment from that establishment. Visa controls in New Zealand are quite stringent, and students will need to get together a number of different documents in order to apply for their student visa.

Students are required to have the following documents in order to be able to apply for a student visa:

1   Offer of a place.
2   Confirmation of Enrolment.
3   General Medical Certificate (INZ 1007) form.
4   Chest X-Ray Certificate (INZ 1096) form.
5   Police certificates to prove you are of good character.
6   Proof of funds for tuition.
7   Proof of funds for living costs: 15,000 NZ$ per year.
8   Proof you intend to leave (e.g. return flight).

Once you have been issued with a student visa you are required to be able to demonstrate that you are passing the course, and if students choose to change their education provider they will need to contact the immigration authorities and let them know.

The student visa will be granted for the period that you have paid for your studies, meaning that students may be required to apply to extend their visa each year. The visa allows students to work over the Christmas and New Year break. Under certain conditions students are also able to work up to 20 hours per week. Students can apply to change the terms of their visa once they are in New Zealand in order to allow them to work the extra 20 hours per week.

Visa applications cost £135 and should be lodged at the following address:
Visa Application Centre
TT Visa Services Ltd
2nd Floor, Mimet House
5A Praed Street
London, W2 1NJ

Contact details:
Website: www.ttsnzvisa.com/
Telephone: 0203 582 7499
E-mail: ttslondonnz@ttepl.com

Student life in New Zealand

Campus life

Students can expect their university experience in New Zealand to be relatively similar to that in the UK in terms of their social life. The legal drinking age in New Zealand is 18 and as in Australia there are no fraternities or sororities, with students instead coming together around shared activities, sports or interests.

The main sports in New Zealand are rugby, cricket and netball. Soccer is also becoming increasingly popular following the Kiwi's first appearance in a World

Cup (South Africa 2010) in 28 years. Students will also find water and winter sports very popular, which is no surprise given New Zealand's spectacular landscape.

New Zealand is the second safest country in the world according to the Global Peace Index (2012), and university campuses usually have security and/or a campus cop who will provide a link to the local police. Students can expect their studies in New Zealand to take place in a safe and friendly atmosphere.

Accommodation and student living

Students have the option to choose between three main types of accommodation in New Zealand: university accommodation (halls of residence), private accommodation or homestay.

Halls of residence and private accommodation will often be comparable in price, with estimates varying between 9,000 NZ$ (£4,800) and 15,000 NZ$ (£8,000) for the full academic year. Students should remember, however, that halls of residence often have the added benefit of including meals. Students may also find that for their first semester, or year, in New Zealand, the option of university accommodation may be the most attractive, as it allows students to mix with other students while they adjust to their new surroundings. Students may find that university accommodation has waiting lists meaning that they may not be able to immediately go into university accommodation upon arrival. Students are also advised to check university websites closely for the closing date of applications to university accommodation.

A private apartment in New Zealand will usually cost between 1,000–1,400 NZ$ (£500–750) per month, but this will depend on a variety of factors, such as the quality of the accommodation, whether students share with other students and the location, both within the city and in the country. Auckland, for example, is notoriously expensive when compared with other New Zealand cities, and students should generally expect to pay more for accommodation and living costs if they are studying there.

The final option is homestay, which will usually work out cheaper for students than either of the other two options. Homestay accommodation provides a safe and easy introduction to life in New Zealand for students, and will include certain meals and other facilities such as laundry. Those interested in homestay accommodation should contact the accommodation or housing departments at their individual universities or search online for agencies linking up students with homestay families.

Healthcare

The New Zealand Government's 'Code of Practice for the Pastoral Care of International Students' requires all international students to have appropriate health and travel insurance while they are residing in the country.

To get an idea of the cost, one popular provider, StudentSafe, charges students 585 NZ$ (£314) per year for health insurance. Students should check the university websites, however, as many universities have 'preferred' providers which they work with and which they might want their students to go through. It is important that students make sure they are familiar with what they are covered for before going out to New Zealand. Students will need to alert the provider to pre-existing conditions, for example, or they may find that they are not covered for expenses relating to that condition.

Further practical information

Transport

Students planning on running a car in New Zealand will need to account for some further expenditures. International drivers are able to drive a car for up to one year on an International Driver's Licence (IDP) or with a driver's licence from their country of origin. However, if you wish to operate a car beyond this year you will need to take a New Zealand driving test, including an eye examination, theory test and driving test.

Running a car in New Zealand is cheaper than it is in the UK, with a gallon of gasoline priced at US$6.73 compared to US$8.06 in the UK. Alternatively you may wish to take public transport while living in New Zealand: a monthly transport pass in most major cities will cost between 90–140 NZ$ (£50–75).

Banking

Setting up a bank account in New Zealand is easy once you have a permanent address. You will need to go down to a branch with your passport in order to set up an account.

Weather

Students should remember that the seasons in New Zealand are the opposite way round to in the UK. This means that students enrolling on programmes in July should expect cold weather upon arrival, while students enrolling in February should expect to be flying out into the end of the summer. Weather in New Zealand is relatively mild, but people will need plenty of warm clothing for the winter.

After you finish your degree

There are a number of visas which international students can apply to if they wish to continue living in New Zealand after graduating from their programme. The two main options available are:

Graduate Job Search visa, which is valid for up to 12 months. This visa is for graduates who do not have a job lined up immediately upon graduation, but who wish to stay in the country and search for a job. Students have to apply no later than three months after completing their degree and need to provide evidence of 4,200 NZ$ to maintain themselves while they search for a job.

Graduate Work Experience visa, which is valid for two years (or in some unique cases three years). This visa is for graduates who have an offer of employment, which is relevant to the qualification they have gained in New Zealand. Students again must apply no later than three months after completing their degree.

Whether or not you choose to stay in New Zealand, students will have had a unique experience living in one of the most beautiful countries in the world and will have internationalised their CV at the same time. International graduates of New Zealand universities will have had the experience of a lifetime, and then can expect to be competitive on the international jobs market afterwards.

Chapter 7

South Africa

Orientation

Introduction

South Africa is one of the largest countries on the continent of Africa, and is the principal African destination for international students. The country's population is a little smaller than the UK, totalling around 50 million people, making South Africa the 24th biggest country worldwide in terms of population. The main cities

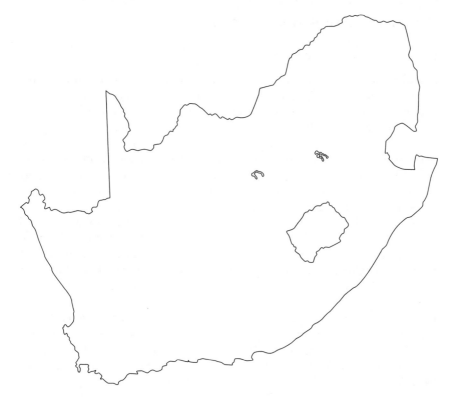

in South Africa are Cape Town, Johannesburg, Durban, Soweto, Pretoria and Port Elizabeth.

There are 11 official languages in South Africa, with different regions having their own local language. Across much of South Africa, English and Afrikaans are also spoken.

IMF Rankings show South Africa to have the biggest economy on the African continent, and the 29th in the world. Despite this, the country still suffers from high rates of unemployment and many people still live in poverty.

Reasons to study in South Africa

- South Africa offers international students more affordable tuition fees than most other English speaking countries.
- South Africa is becoming an increasingly popular destination for UK postgraduate students because of the quality of research in specialised fields.
- Living costs in South Africa are much more affordable than they are in other possible international destinations for UK students.
- South Africa is a place of astonishing natural beauty, and can provide an astounding backdrop to student's higher education.

Higher education in South Africa

Finding your course and institution

There are 23 public universities and 18 private universities in South Africa. Of the public universities, 11 are traditional universities (offering typical university degrees), six are technological (offering vocational degrees), and six are comprehensive (offering a combination of the two). Students will find that the private universities are often specialised, becoming business schools or film schools for example. An early choice thus needs to be made by international students looking at studying in South Africa as regards to what type of institution they should apply to. The type of programme students are interested in studying will dictate which universities are open to them.

South Africa is becoming one of the most popular destinations for international students, with over 60,000 international students currently studying in the country. Many of the international students come from SADC (South African Development Community) countries, but increasing numbers of UK students are also travelling to South Africa in search of affordable higher education. Universities like the University of Cape Town, University of Pretoria and North-West University are becoming accustomed to enrolling high numbers of international students each year, particularly at a postgraduate level. The South African academic calendar is similar to that in Australia and New Zealand, with the first semester running from February until June and the second running from July until November.

South African universities are beginning to be recognised at a world level for their quality of teaching and research, and many can be found in world rankings such as the QS World University Rankings or Times Higher Education University World Rankings. The highest ranked in both is the University of Cape Town which comes in at 154th and 113th respectively.

The credit system

A credit system is employed across public universities in South Africa as part of the National Qualifications Framework (NQF) allowing students to easily transfer between courses and universities. A standard yearly credit load in South Africa is 120 credits, meaning that students are required to complete 360 credits to graduate from a three-year Bachelor's degree.

Many universities award their degrees in the same classifications as UK universities, awarding degrees ranging from 1st Class to 3rd Class.

Financing your studies

Tuition fees and living costs

Tuition fees

Tuition fees in South Africa for international students are less expensive than those in many other English speaking countries. Tuition for undergraduate programmes often ranges between 25,000–50,000 Rand, which is equivalent to between £1,700–3,500. Note that 1.0 South African Rand is equal to £0.07 at the time of writing. Master's degree programmes are usually similarly priced, more regularly costing in the upper bracket of that range.

International students will find that tuition is often expressed as an average price of the programme. This is because the actual price of tuition depends on which modules are taken, with each module having a different assigned price. Universities will also often have two prices for international students, one for students from the SADC and another for all other international students. The SADC are 15 countries in Southern Africa, and students from this region receive discounted tuition rates, sometimes the same as South African students. Students from all other nations will pay the same international tuition fee rate. Please note that sometimes tuition fees are charged in American Dollars rather than in Rand (the local currency).

Students should also note that some universities charge international students additional administrative levies which may cost as much as £150. Students should check carefully with the website of each university they apply for to make sure they are aware of any extra costs they may be required to pay.

Living costs

Aside from the tuition fees, you need to consider the price of living in South Africa while pursuing your studies. Table 7.1 provides a rough guide for further living expenses in South Africa.

Financial aid

Some universities in South Africa offer scholarships to academically gifted students, but often these are limited to postgraduate students. Students would be advised to also seek out financial aid from non-university organisations. The Commonwealth Scholarship Commission, for example, awards scholarships to UK students studying abroad, and in South Africa this is available to Master's degree students as well as PhD students. Those interested in studying a Master's degree in South Africa should consult the following website to see whether they might be eligible, and to inform themselves about the application process: www.cscuk. dfid.gov.uk/apply/scholarships-uk-citizens/south-africa/.

Table 7.1 Cost of living in South Africa

Cost	Price
Application fees	Most universities charge international students an application fee, which ranges between 100–350 Rand (approximately £7–25).
Accommodation	Accommodation costs will depend on a variety of factors such as whether you choose university accommodation and where in the country you are studying. Estimates can range between 2,000–3,750 Rand per month (approximately £140–260). For more information please see the 'Student life in South Africa' section.
Living costs	Halls of residence offering students food will often charge extra for this service, frequently costing as much as the accommodation does itself. Otherwise, the University of Cape Town, for example, states that students should budget 2,000 Rand for food monthly (approximately £140).
Books and supplies	Books and supplies can cost as much as 5,000 Rand per semester, according to some university quotas (approximately £350). However, these costs can sometimes be brought down by purchasing second hand and making good use of library facilities.
Health	Health insurance can typically cost between 3,000–4,000 Rand per month (approximately £210–280).
Other costs	Additional expenses such as social expenses, transport, mobile phone bills and travelling between semesters will depend largely on the student. A conservative budget of 2,000 Rand per semester should be given (approximately £140).

Student loans

Unlike in many other countries, international students are in some cases able to apply for student loans to help fund their studies in South Africa. All of South Africa's major banks offer student loans to both international and national students, including Absa Bank, Nedbank, First National Bank and Standard Bank. Students applying for the loan will be required to be already enrolled upon the programme and will need a sponsor (e.g. their parents) to be a signatory for them. The sponsor will need to show that they have a good credit history and have a record of gainful employment for the last few years.

Applying to your universities

Application process

The deadline for students applying to enrol in Semester 1 is usually in September or October. However, students will need to begin the application process well before this as most universities require several documents to be attached to applications, including certified copies of their academic documents to date. Applications can usually be made either online or by post; however, those applying by post must remember to leave ample time for their application to arrive before the deadline.

As A Level students do not receive their A Level certificates until November or December, South African universities will often require all undergraduate students to apply using their AS Level results, predicted grades or indeed A Level results slip, and then present the certificate to the university once it has been released. For information about this you should contact each different university's admissions or International Office to find out their process.

Application forms will usually require information about your academic and professional career to date and will sometimes require references and/or a personal statement. Halls of residence application forms are often contained within the university application form, meaning that both are done at once. Graduates will be required to also attach certified copies of their academic transcripts and in some cases will need to provide a research proposal.

Visa information

Study permits

To apply for a student visa you will need:

1 An official letter of acceptance from a South African university.
2 Medical and radiological reports.
3 Your passport.

4 Two passport sized photographs.
5 Proof of valid medical insurance. (For more information see the 'Student life in South Africa' section.)
6 Details about your accommodation plans.
7 A police clearance certificate.
8 A correctly filled in application form.
9 Proof of sufficient funds to cover tuition and living expenses.
10 A £600 security (or repatriation) deposit, which is used to guarantee you will be able to return home at the end of your course of studies.

Students applying for a study permit will also be required to pay the processing fee which is £35. Note that this fee may change, and students should consult the website below which will list up to date information about the application process including the application fee. The applications usually take around six weeks to process, so students should allow at least six weeks between when they apply and when they intend to begin their programme.

All enquiries about visa applications should be made to the South African High Commission – contact information can be found below:

South African High Commission
South Africa House
9 Duncannon Street
Trafalgar Square
London, WC2N 5DP
Website: www.southafricahouseuk.com/visas/vis_forcit.html
Telephone number: 02079258920

Student life in South Africa

Campus life

Studying abroad in South Africa is likely to be a bigger challenge for UK students than studying in some other popular foreign destinations. However, the bigger difference in culture and lifestyle between South Africa and the UK may well end up meaning that UK students find their time in South Africa a much more rewarding experience.

Despite these differences, there is a lot of variety available in South African university life. For those students who want it, a busy social life and nightlife can be found, particularly in the bigger cities. South Africa is also a very sporting country, and international students will find many opportunities to engage in university sports. The most popular sports in South Africa are football, rugby and cricket, but students will not be limited to these options alone. Students should be warned that registration week in South African universities can be a very stressful experience, and it can often take students several weeks to organise a timetable for themselves which does not have their different programmes clashing. As long as students are prepared for this to take time, then they should not worry.

Safety remains a key issue in South Africa, and international students are advised to take every precaution available to keep themselves and their belongings secure. Having said that, if students are sensible and aware of the safety issues that exist in South Africa, they can expect to have a fantastic university experience; indeed, there are thousands of international students studying in South Africa and thoroughly enjoying their time there.

Universities themselves will often have a variety of measures in place, and can help international students be aware of what is safe to do and what isn't. All campuses, for example, will have 24/7 security and an on-campus doctor. Students who are out late around campus, using the library facilities for example, will be able to (and are advised to) use a campus escort service by the campus police to accompany them back to their student accommodation.

Universities will also be able to recommend which taxi services should be used when getting around the city, and advise on the best way of getting around. In general it is advisable to take taxis after it gets dark.

If students make sure to follow the advice given to them, they will find that student life in South Africa can be a thoroughly rewarding experience. For those who are interested there are a diverse range of volunteering programmes which international students can take part in part-time alongside their studies. Many international students also take advantage of the summer break to travel around South Africa, which is a country of astounding natural beauty. Students are advised, however, to make sure to try and travel with other students or friends for their own safety.

Accommodation and student living

Students in South Africa can choose between halls of residence and private accommodation. However, in the interest of safety it would be advisable for first time students to opt for the former for when they arrive. Students may then choose to move out in the following years once they have acclimatised to the country and know which areas would be safe to live in and which wouldn't.

Most halls of residence applications are made at the same time as applying for your programme. Fees for halls of residence are usually a little cheaper than suitable private accommodation as well, varying between around 16,000–22,000 Rand per year (approximately £1,100–1,500). Students should remember that food is not usually included in these prices, and is usually charged extra, usually costing the same as the accommodation does. Those who are not eating in their halls of residence will need to remember to budget around 2,000 Rand (£140) for their monthly shopping bill.

Healthcare

As in most countries, international students studying in South Africa are required to have health insurance in order to be allowed a student visa. The health insurance will need to be one taken out in South Africa and which is recognised by the South African Government. The following website will provide students with a list of medical schemes available for students: www.medicalschemes.com/Medical Schemes.aspx/.

Students will find, however, that the International Office at the university you intend to study will most likely provide you with guidance on which medical scheme to go for. To give a general idea of the price, Student Health Plan, one of the medical scheme providers in South Africa, prices their medical scheme at between 3,000–4,000 Rand (£210–280) per year.

Work while you study

International students are able to work part-time for no more than 20 hours per week on their study permit. For those who need to work more than this amount as part of their course, they are required to apply for further permission from Home Affairs to be able to do so.

Further practical information

Mobile phones

A cheap mobile phone will cost students around 250 Rand (approximately £17). Most mobile phone contracts in South Africa are a minimum of two years in length, so students may choose to go for pay-as-you-go plans which do not tie them down long term. A pay-as-you-go starter pack can cost around 10 Rand (approximately £0.70). The main four network providers are: Vodacom, MTN, Cell C and Tellcom.

Banking

International students are able to open accounts at most banks with their study permits. Banks will usually require you to bring your passport, study permit and information about your permanent address in South Africa in order to open an account. Under 25s/26s are often able to open specific student accounts with added benefits for students studying at university. For details about what each bank offers, you should check their individual websites. Examples of some of the main banks in South Africa are: FNB, Standard Bank, Absa, Nedbank and Post Bank.

Transport

A monthly transport pass can cost students between 300–700 Rand (approximately £20–50), although student discounts may be available in certain cities. Students are unlikely to need cars if they are living in halls of residence which are usually located on campus. Cars are available for rent, however, should you wish to use one during the summer holidays for example. A gallon of gasoline in South Africa currently costs US$5.06 as compared to US$8.06 in the UK.

After you finish your degree

Students intending to remain in South Africa after their degree are required to have an offer of employment in order to apply for a visa allowing them to stay. This means that students will need to begin searching for work before completing their degree, as once the degree is complete the study permit allowing students to remain in South Africa will expire quite quickly.

For those who return to the UK, or indeed look for gainful employment elsewhere in the world, they should be able to look back on their time in South Africa as a truly remarkable experience. This, alongside a considerably smaller student debt (if they have one at all) and an internationalised CV, should mean that graduates of South African universities are in a good position to embark on their post-university careers.

Chapter 8

Ireland

Orientation

Introduction

The Republic of Ireland has a population of 4.7 million people. The major cities are Dublin (1.1 million); Cork (200,000); Limerick (90,000); Galway (80,000); and Waterford (50,000). Over 90 per cent of the population are practising Roman Catholics and the country has two official languages: English and Irish. Irish (Gaelic) is spoken mainly in areas located along the western seaboard and has about 83,000 native speakers. The unit of currency is the Euro.

Ireland gained independence from the United Kingdom on 6 December 1921. Ireland is a Republic with a President as chief of state. In the 1990s it experienced an economic boom but since 2008 had an economic crisis caused mainly by a banking crisis and a slump in property prices. In 2010, the Government negotiated an assistance package with the EU and IMF which has helped to keep vital public services running. The Government has implemented banking sector reform, fiscal consolidation and structural reforms, and there are signs that these are beginning to bring about a positive change.

Ireland today has a worldwide reputation for its culture and its cultural achievements. For a comparatively small island, it has made a disproportionately large contribution to world literature (Jonathan Swift, Oscar Wilde, William Butler Yeats, James Joyce and Samuel Becket, to name just some, are world-renowned writers) demonstrating the high levels of education in Ireland.

Reasons to study in Ireland

- UK students are not charged tuition fees to study in the Republic of Ireland (although they do have to pay an annual student services fee).
- Ireland is one of the only other countries in Europe where English is the first language, meaning UK students will not encounter language barriers.
- Ireland is well connected to most UK airports with cheap budget airline flights, making travelling back and forth between home and university much easier.

- Ireland is a country of astounding natural beauty (nicknamed the Emerald Isle).
- The quality of higher education is internationally recognised.
- Irish culture is in many ways similar to British culture, and UK students will have a similar university experience to that of UK universities.

Higher education in Ireland

Finding your course and institution

Higher education in the Republic of Ireland experienced large growth up until the economic crisis, with over 10,000 international students enrolling in full-time higher education programmes in Ireland in 2012. Of these, 1,162 were from the UK, making British students one of the largest international student groups in Ireland. Indeed, Ireland is the most popular European destination for UK students.

There are many higher education institutions in the Republic of Ireland including the following seven public universities:

University	Website
University College Cork (National University of Ireland, Cork)	www.ucc.ie/en/international/
University College Dublin (National University of Ireland, Dublin)	www.ucd.ie/international/
National University of Ireland, Galway	www.nuigalway.ie/international-students/
National University of Ireland, Maynooth	http://international.nuim.ie/
Trinity College Dublin	www.tcd.ie/international/
Dublin City University	www.dcu.ie/international/index.shtml
University of Limerick	www.ul.ie/international/

Students will also find a wide variety of private higher education institutions in Ireland. These can vary in specialisation and size from Burton College of Art (200 students) to Dublin Business School (9,000 students). Apart from universities, institutes of technology (of which there are 14) are another form of higher education offered. These further education institutions were created from the late 1960s onwards. Originally they offered only National Certificates and Diploma courses, particularly in the fields of Business, Engineering and Science, but they have now developed to offer full Bachelor's, Master's and Doctoral programmes. For more information about the Institute of Technology and the programmes they offer please consult the following website: www.ioti.ie/.

There are over 2,500 courses available in Ireland for international students to choose from, so narrowing down your choice can be a daunting process. The following website may provide a useful starting point, particularly its search function, where students can search through universities by course and location: www.educationinireland.com/en/.

Though decisions should in no way be made by world academic ranking alone, it may interest students to know that three Irish universities are included in the QS World University Rankings top 200: Trinity College Dublin (67), University College Dublin (131) and University College Cork (190).

Financing your studies

Tuition fees and living costs

Tuition fees

For UK/EU students, tuition is free in the Republic of Ireland and is met in full by the Exchequer. This falls under the 'Free Fees Initiative'. There are, however, certain conditions for this to apply:

- Studies must be for a minimum of two years duration.
- You cannot study for a second undergraduate qualification or already have a postgraduate qualification.
- If you fail a year you will need to pay to repeat the year (unless you have good medical grounds for this).

Note: There is an obligatory 'Student Services Charge' (equivalent to a registration fee). This is currently €2,500 and set to rise to €3,000 by 2015. You may also need to pay a capitation fee (this may be a couple of hundred Euros for student clubs and societies).

Living costs

Table 8.1 gives the general living costs for Ireland.

Student loans

UK students (apart from those from Northern Ireland) are not entitled to UK student loans and maintenance grants/loans for studying in the Republic of Ireland. However, there is currently a means-tested maintenance grant available for Northern Irish students planning on studying in the Republic of Ireland (for further information visit: www.studentfinanceni.co.uk/).

Applying to your universities

Time frame

There are two application deadlines: 1 February for normal applications and 1 May for late applications. Some courses have restricted application (these are ones that

Table 8.1 Cost of living in Ireland

Cost	Price
Application fees	EU students should apply through the Central Applications Office (CAO). This will cost students between €40–80 depending on when they submit their application, and whether they do so online or by post.
Accommodation	On-campus accommodation in the form of halls of residence will typically cost between €400–600 per month. Private accommodation is more variable in price (depending on quality, and location) and can cost anywhere between €300–700 per month.
Basic living costs	A typical monthly food bill in Ireland is estimated as being around €200, while students might expect to pay around €100 in utilities and bills (if they are living in private accommodation).
Books and supplies	Students should allow €500 per year for books and supplies.
Health insurance	EU students do not need to take out health insurance to study in other EU countries such as Ireland, but can instead use their European Health Insurance Card (EHIC) cards.
Extra living costs	Travel and social expenses will largely depend on the lifestyle of the student and the city they are studying in, but an average of €200 per month should be allowed.

fill quickly) and these can only be applied for by 1 February. Universities normally list their restricted courses on their websites.

Application procedure

The Republic of Ireland operates a central application system similar to UCAS for applications from EU/EEA students. It is called the Central Applications Office (CAO). Note that it is, however, the higher education institutions that retain decision making for acceptance to their programmes.

EU students should apply for full-time undergraduate courses at Irish universities/higher education institutions through the CAO. The CAO provides an applications pack with a handbook which lists all the courses on offer and gives information on how to apply.

Note: There is an application fee payable to the CAO. The fee rate corresponds to the closing dates: if you apply by the closing date of 1 February the fee is currently €40; if you make a late application (by 1 May) it is €50 for an online application and €80 for a paper application.

The CAO may be contacted at:

Central Applications Office
Tower House
Eglington Street
Galway
Tel: +353 91 509800
Fax: +353 91 562344
Website: www.cao.ie/

Recognition of your qualifications

The following is a useful website for you to check your qualifications in terms of equivalencies with the Irish education system: www.qualificationsrecognition.ie/qualification-recognition-service-database.html.

The final examination in the Irish secondary school system is called the Leaving Certificate Examination (commonly referred to as the Leaving Cert.). It is completed after two (or sometimes three) years of preparation in the senior cycle at school. Irish students study more subjects between the ages of 16–18 than UK students as the Leaving Certificate requires a minimum of five subjects to be examined, with many students taking six or seven. Each subject may be examined at Higher (HL), Ordinary (OL) or Foundation (FL) levels. Table 8.2 outlines the Irish Leaving Certificate grades to points.

In Ireland, a number of points ranging between 0 and 100 are awarded to the student for each Leaving Certificate exam sat. Students then combine the points from their six top scoring exams, which gives a final total score between 0 and 600. A maximum of 100 points can be achieved in each subject at Higher Level

Table 8.2 Irish Leaving Certificate grades to points

Grade	% range	Points at HL	Points at OL	Points at FL
A1	90–100	100	60	20
A2	85–89	90	50	15
B1	80–84	85	45	10
B2	75–79	80	40	5
B3	70–74	75	35	0
C1	65–69	70	30	0
C2	60–64	65	25	0
C3	55–59	60	20	0
D1	50–54	55	15	0
D2	45–49	50	10	0
D3	40–44	45	5	0

Table 8.3 Comparison between A Level
grades and the Irish Leaving
Certificate points

A Level grade	Equivalent Irish Leaving Certificate points (CAO points)
A*	150
A	135
B	120
C	100
D	75
E	40
AS Level grade	
A	65
B	60
C	50
D	35
E	20

(60 points at Ordinary Level and 20 points at Foundation Level). Universities state the number of points and the subjects they require these points in for entry to their programmes. For guidance, you can compare A Level grades to these points in Table 8.3.

This chart is a rough guide for you and you can use it to get an idea of what you need to achieve in your A Levels. It means, for example, that if you are offered a place at an Irish university conditional upon obtaining 390 CAO points you will need to get, for example, two A grades and one B grade at A Level (or two A* grades and a C grade).

Each university sets its own entry requirements and these may vary from year to year subject to demand. University websites will help you in determining what you require.

Student life in Ireland

Campus life

University life in Ireland is comparable to that in the UK, with a wide variety of social activities, sports and societies and associations for students to get involved in.

Accommodation and student living

Students usually have the choice between on-campus accommodation provided by the university and private accommodation. On-campus accommodation is in high demand, and as a result can be slightly more costly than private accommodation. However, this depends on the city, as private accommodation prices are variable across Ireland and will be considerably higher for example in Dublin (which is notoriously expensive) than in some of the smaller more provincial towns and cities.

As a general rule, students can expect to pay between €400–600 per month for on-campus accommodation, and between €300–700 per month for private accommodation. The price of private accommodation will depend on a variety of factors, including the quality, whether you share with other students and the location (both in the city and in the country).

Most universities will have accommodation offices which will be able to help you, not only with on-campus accommodation, but with information about private rentals in the surrounding areas. Many will work directly with local estate agents and landlords and will be able to give you some tips and ideas about prices.

Food and socialising are not cheap in Ireland (particularly in Dublin), and a minimum of €400 per month should be factored in for these costs. The Irish Council for International Students recommends a minimum of €8,000–12,000 for living costs (including accommodation) in Ireland per year, with Dublin being at the upper end of that estimate.

Healthcare

UK students, as in the rest of Europe, are covered by their European Health Insurance Card (EHIC). EU students are subsequently not required to take out any private health insurance to study in Ireland.

Work while you study

As there are no issues with visas for EU citizens wishing to study and/or work in other EU countries, UK students will be able to work during their studies in Ireland just as they would be able to in the UK. Some universities themselves may put limits on the amount that students are allowed to work during term time however. Students should contact the university International Office to enquire.

Students should note, however, that it may not be very easy to find employment in Ireland right away as (at the time of writing) the country is experiencing stagnated growth and high levels of unemployment, making jobs harder to come by. Students who are able to secure a job, however, will find that wages in Ireland are usually quite high.

Further practical information

Driving

UK students wishing to run a car while they are studying in Ireland will find that they are able to use their UK driving licence until it expires without needing to take out an Irish driving licence. The cost of running a car will be comparable to UK prices, with a gallon of gasoline costing US$8.05 in Ireland and US$8.06 in the UK (in 2013).

Mobile phone

There are a variety of mobile network providers in Ireland, such as Vodafone Ireland, O2, 3, Tesco Mobile Ireland and eMobile. Prices for a monthly plan are comparable to UK prices, and will depend on the terms of the monthly package.

After you finish your degree

Students will find that their degrees from Irish universities will leave them as competitive in the European jobs market as the equivalent UK qualifications would. However, with the added benefit of no student debt, and the experience of having lived in another country, students may find themselves in a better position than many other UK graduates.

Chapter 9

Europe

Orientation

Introduction

The European Union (EU) is comprised of 28 member countries. The founding members in 1951 were France, West Germany, Belgium, Italy, Luxembourg and the Netherlands (who formed the then EEC). The UK joined in 1973. The most

recent to join in 2004 are: Estonia, Latvia, Lithuania, Poland, Czech Republic, Slovakia, Slovenia, Cyprus, Malta and Hungary; and in 2007: Romania and Bulgaria. The most recent country to join is Croatia in 2013.

The European Economic Area (EEA) is comprised of the 28 EU member states as well as Norway, Iceland and Lichtenstein. Switzerland is not in the EEA but has many special agreements with the EEA that make it, to all intents and purposes, similar to a member state for access to its education system for UK students. The EEA countries tend to follow the same open access to their university education systems as the EU members.

There are 23 official languages in the EU and many more actual languages in use across Europe. The main divide is between the Romance languages of the South (derived from Latin) and the Germanic languages of the North and Slavic languages of the East. There are other language groups such as the Finno-Ugric group (Hungarian, Estonian and Finnish) and Celtic derived languages that are found, for example, within the British Isles, or regional languages such as Basque, Catalan and Galician within the Spanish peninsular. The picture is complex with national borders not necessarily matching language boundaries. Given this complexity it is not surprising that the *de facto lingua franca*, particularly among the young, is English. This, however, does not mean that English is understood evenly across the continent.

The population of the EU is just over 500 million, with Germany being the most populated country with over 80 million, followed by the larger nations of the UK, France and Italy which all have over 60 million. Because of the colonial legacy of many European countries and the (until recently) economic attractiveness of the continent, the populations of Europe have become increasingly multicultural.

Economically the EU is currently experiencing problems with a negative GDP (-0.2 per cent) and high youth unemployment, which is particularly accentuated in the southern states. Structural reforms are being implemented in a number of countries and there is a polemic as to whether these are aiding recovery or not.

Reasons to study in Europe

- Tuition fees are cheap, often being free for EU students.
- The quality of education is good (excluding the UK there are 52 universities across the EU in the top 200 according to the Times Higher Education World Rankings 2012–13).
- Increasingly, programmes are taught in English at both undergraduate and postgraduate levels.
- The continent is easily accessible from the UK, particularly with the rise of many low-cost airlines linking up European cities.
- Europe is by and large a safe place to live.
- EU citizens are not required to acquire a visa to study or work in other EU countries.
- You are covered for medical insurance by your EHIC card.

- You have the possibility of learning other useful world languages and discovering other cultures as a value added bonus to your studies.

Higher education in Europe

The EU states have put in place a system of agreement for the mutual recognition of each other's university education systems and awards: the Bologna Declaration. This was signed by 29 European countries in 1999. The Lisbon Treaty in 2007 further cemented this process. These agreements seek to create ease of mobility for educational purposes between the citizens of the member states of the EU and to develop a mutually understandable and uniform European Higher Education Area (EHEA). The cornerstone of these agreements is that in effect all citizens of members states should be able to study in any member country's higher education system on the same terms as each country's own citizens. In other words, a UK student has the right to access any EU university on the same conditions and financial terms (for tuition fees) as the local people of that EU member state country.

The Bologna Declaration has also promoted the standardisation of the higher education system across the member states. A higher education system of Bachelor's degrees, Master's degrees and Doctoral degrees at universities has been established, with a regular Bachelor's degree (also known as the Licence or 'L' level) being three years in duration, the Master's (also known as 'M' level) degree being two years in duration and the Doctoral degree (PhD or 'D' level) being three years of study. The Lisbon Treaty further developed this idea by instigating a common credit system (The European Credit Transfer System) as shown in Table 9.1.

Although the standard Bachelor's degree is awarded after 180 ECTS credits have been gained, certain professional degrees, such as Engineering, are often four years in duration, i.e. they are awarded after 240 credits worth of study have been gained. Medical degrees are usually five years (Dentistry) or six years (General Medicine) and include a year of hospital placement practice. Credits are also awarded increasingly across degrees for work placements or placements overseas. Many programmes in Europe take this aspect of their degree seriously, requiring students to take up to 30 credits worth of work placement during their studies.

Table 9.1 Division of higher education studies with associated credits

Level of study	Year		European Credits (ECTS)
Bachelor's degree (L)	1	First cycle	60
	2		60
	3		60
			Total = 180
Master's degree (M)	1	Second cycle	60
	2		60
			Total = 120

Because in the UK a Master's degree usually only lasts one year (including the summer when students write their dissertations), the UK Master's degree is usually awarded with 90 M-level ECTS.

Traditionally, many countries have not operated a Bachelor/Master's (L/M) distinction. A university degree was awarded only after completing five years of study. In countries such as Denmark and Holland, higher education has been divided between universities with a professional educational focus, i.e. vocational universities (in Holland these are the universities of Applied Science) and research universities.

Note: The degrees awarded by the vocational universities (professional degrees), which normally require up to four years of study, do not allow for automatic access to Master's degree programmes in the research universities. This is different to the UK system where a clear progression between a Bachelor's degree awarded by all universities and a Master's degree at other universities is offered across the sector.

Semesters and grading

Semesters usually run from September to the end of January and from February to the end of June. There are usually examinations at the end of each semester and university transcripts reflect the grades achieved at the end of each semester. This means a transcript will have six sets of results for a full three-year degree.

Finding your course and institution

The choice across Europe is vast and so knowing where to start on your search may seem rather bewildering. This section therefore offers you a methodology for honing your search.

The first issue is deciding what you would like to study. Once you have an idea of the subject area you wish to pursue then the other factors of location (which country or countries you are interested in living and studying in) and cost (how much you are prepared and able to spend on your studies) become key factors in narrowing down your search.

Useful websites to help you with your search are:

www.studyineurope.eu/
http://eacea.ec.europa.eu/education/eurydice/
http://europa.eu/

Two areas that attract students to study in Europe are the English taught Medicine and Dentistry programmes on offer (Italy, Central and Eastern Europe) and at postgraduate level the range of private business schools offering MBAs (Masters of Business Administration). It is also worth noting that specific countries have developed specialisms and strengths in certain areas, for example Switzerland is famous for its Hotel and Hospitality Management programmes and Germany has a name for Engineering.

Generally speaking, students will find that there are more programmes being taught in English at postgraduate level than undergraduate level, particularly in the sciences and arts and humanities.

Studying medical programmes in Europe

Eastern and Central European medical universities are growing in popularity due to their programmes in Medicine (six years), Dentistry (five years) and Veterinary Medicine (six years) which are taught in English. In Western Europe, there are not many such programmes on offer, with the exception of Italy, which is beginning to offer full six-year programmes in English for Medicine as well.

Fees vary, with state universities in Italy and Romania being the cheapest and much cheaper than the UK. Application requirements vary, and it may be possible to find entry applications in some that are lower than those currently required in the UK. In fact, there are thousands of applicants for Medicine in the UK each year that are not able to gain a place and so the EU medical universities that teach in English may provide an attractive alternative. They are also an attractive option as graduates are able to apply to register with the GMC (General Medical Council) and the GDC (General Dental Council) without having to sit any further examinations.

Application procedures also vary, with some universities requiring entrance examinations (the IMAT for Italian medical universities, or individual university examinations in some other cases). These are usually in multiple choice formats and usually cover the areas of Biology and Chemistry, and sometimes Physics or Maths. Other universities require you to submit your end of high school examination results (A Levels/IB) – some requiring legalised copies of these. The number of places that universities can offer is usually controlled by the Ministry of Education (MoE) in that country.

Private universities and business schools

There are two types of universities or higher education establishments in Europe: private sector and public sector. The public sector must abide by the regulations of the state and allow equal access to its universities for all EU students on the same terms as home students. Private sector universities and business schools are not bound by such regulations and charge market driven fees. Europe, in competition with the USA, is becoming an attractive location for postgraduate students wishing to study for an MBA in English. The advantages are the comparatively lower cost, the quality of education and the added bonus of experiencing another language and culture.

Note: Private universities, because they depend on the income of their students to survive, tend to be much more efficient and simple with their application procedures.

Because private universities are independent of the state, you need to check the regulatory bodies that validate/accredit the degrees offered by these universities. In many cases the MoE may not recognise or validate the degrees they offer. This may not be because the degrees are not worthy of being considered equivalent to state-awarded degrees, but may be down to administrative or political reasons. For this reason you will find that many private universities which are not able to offer state recognition of their degrees rely on private sector regulation and validation – a business school in France, for example, may offer International Assembly for Collegiate Business Education (IACBE) accreditation. These organisations are often based in the USA. Different accreditation boards have different statuses: the AACSB is for top US Business Schools, EQUIS for European Business Schools. For private universities/business schools it is prudent and easy for you to check out their accreditations.

The credit system

One potential difference that exists between the EU and the UK university systems is the university credit system. UK universities are regulated by the Quality Standards Agency (QSA) and the QSA recommends that all programmes offered by universities in England and Wales need to have Intended Learning Outcomes (ILOs), which students are assessed on before they are awarded credits.

A three-year programme needs to show a progression as reflected in each year's ILOs, so that credits are awarded according to each year's level of study. Year 1 of university study is called Level 4 (in the National Qualifications' Framework for England and Wales – Scotland has its own framework), Year 2 is Level 5 and Year 3 is Level 6. The level of study of a Master's degree is Level 7. This in effect means that a student must pass credits at the right levels to be able to progress in their studies. This is not necessarily the case in the rest of the EHEA, where students are required to gain 180 credits at First Cycle/Bachelor's ('L') level to obtain a Bachelor's degree. For this reason students may be able to take any courses from each year in any order to obtain their degree. There is, however, a movement towards having an ILO system in EU countries which is similar in ethos to that in the UK.

Pre-requisites: In the UK you may need to study a course at Level 4 before being able to study a course at Level 5, when on a Bachelor's degree. The Level 4 course is a pre-requisite for the Level 5 course. Pre-requisites may not exist on programmes in other EU university degree programmes.

How to convert UK University Credits to the ECTS:
2 UK University Credit (CATS) = 1 ECTS

Financing your studies

Tuition fees and living costs

Tuition fees

With the increase in UK university tuition fees to up to £9,000 per year of study at Bachelor's level, the fact that the UK is a member of the EU and a signatory to the Bologna Declaration takes on a special significance. Studying in EU member countries looks increasingly attractive as UK university fees rise.

As EU/EEA citizens, UK students are able to access EU member states' universities on the same fee terms as the citizens of those states. For example, currently in Denmark, university education is free to its citizens (at both under-graduate and postgraduate level), and so it is also free to UK students as well. In Holland there is a tuition fee (currently below €2,000 per year) and so a UK student can study in Holland by paying this amount of tuition fee. Because of the importance of equal access terms to the university, as a UK citizen in principle you have the right to obtain tuition fee loans from any EU country governments which offer them to their own students. In Italy, for example, there is a means-tested system of loans available to all EU students. This, however, is complex to access as eligibility is based on merit and means testing. In Holland, where the tuition fees are quite modest, there is a loans system in place for EU students as well.

Tuition fee levels vary across Europe. There are ten countries in which there are no tuition fees applicable for UK students (as members of the EU/EEA). These are: Sweden, Norway, Denmark, Finland, Greece, Malta, Cyprus, Austria, Germany and Ireland (which has its own section in this guide). Other countries do charge fees, but these are significantly lower than the UK, which has the most expensive tuition fees in the EU/EEA.

It is worth noting that in some countries different universities in different regions charge different fees, adding to the complexity. In Germany, for example, many universities are scrapping their recently introduced tuition fees and so there are now many free universities, although depending on the politics of the region, some still do charge fees (these are, however, relatively low). In other countries such as France, the tuition and registration fees are again low, but they are standardised and controlled across the country.

In many countries across Europe, where the primary language is not an internationally spoken one, programmes are often offered in English as well as in the local language. This is done so that universities in those countries are able to attract international students who would otherwise be put off by having to learn the local language. The advantage of this is that UK students are able to study programmes at universities across the whole of Europe. However, the disadvantage is that when teaching in a non-local language, universities are able to charge higher tuition fees, which they often do (particularly in Central and Eastern Europe). Thus, studying Medicine in Bulgarian, for example, will be cheaper than studying

Medicine in English (in Bulgaria). It is worth noting, however, that these higher fees are usually still cheaper than UK tuition rates. Local students wishing to study in English will also have to pay the higher rates.

Living costs

Just as tuition fee levels vary across the EU/EEA, so does the cost of living. Generally in Northern Europe, the cost of living is high. It is lower in the South and substantially lower in the East. Whereas a sum of £1,000 per month is needed in Denmark for living costs (accommodation, food, etc.), only some £400 is needed in Bulgaria for the same. It is also worth bearing in mind that the cost of living in capital and major cities is substantially more than in the smaller provincial towns.

Financial aid

It may be worth checking with certain bodies if they can offer loans. For postgraduate loans the Skills Funding Agency (SFA) (http://skillsfundingagency. bis.gov.uk/) offer information on Professional and Career Development Loans offered commercially by two UK banks. However, there are a number of conditions attached to securing these loans for study abroad (the provider must be registered with the SFA or be prepared to register; the programme you wish to study must not be available as an equivalent in the UK; and, of course, the bank must be satisfied that the applicant has a satisfactory credit history to be offered the loan).

Securing financial backing to undertake study abroad in Europe is not usually a possibility. There are exceptions to this, however: Bulgaria operates a commercial loans system through a private bank for EU students, and Holland allows EU students to apply for additional maintenance support if they are under 30 years of age and have had a job working 30 hours per week for over three months (i.e. once they have contributed to the economy).

In France you may be able to apply to the regional government for assistance with your accommodation costs through APL (Aide Personalisée au Logement), which is the rent subsidy scheme run by the CAF (Caisse d'Allocations Familiales).

It is a good idea to spend time researching what is available and how you can apply for it in the country you choose to study in. But be aware that in general, the situation in Europe effectively means that while tuition fees may be much less than in the UK, or indeed study may be free, UK students do need to seriously consider how they will meet the living costs of studying in another EU country.

Student loans

As a rule of thumb national governments do not offer maintenance loans to non-nationals of their own countries. This means that a UK student will need to factor in the cost of living in an EU country and realise this is an expense that has to be met out of their own pocket. This is not the case for UK students who study in the UK as they can apply for maintenance loans from the Student Loans Company (SLC) and also be in receipt of maintenance grants should they meet the means-testing criteria.

Note that whereas some governments allow their national student loan facility to be used by students to study in other countries, the UK does not currently allow students to do this.

Remember that when studying in the EU:

- You **can't** be required to pay **higher course fees** than local people.
- You're entitled to the same **grants to cover course fees** as nationals of the country. (This may or may not be the case if the programme is taught in English however.)

Erasmus academic exchange programmes

One way to have the study abroad experience in Europe is to take part in the Erasmus academic exchange programme. This is administered in the UK by the British Council. The exchange is for students who are currently on an undergraduate programme in a UK university. The countries that participate in the programme are 33 in total. These include all 28 EU member countries, Switzerland, Liechtenstein, Iceland, The Former Yugoslav Republic of Macedonia and Turkey.

In order to be able to be selected by your UK university, the university needs to have drawn up a bilateral agreement with a partner university in the scheme for student mobility. This is relatively easy to achieve and most UK universities have a dedicated Erasmus coordinator responsible for this who you can discuss this possibility with.

The Erasmus scheme, in which some 8,000 UK students participate each year, is a great opportunity for you to spend between 3 and 12 months of your studies in another partner country university and have your studies there recognised and credited back into your UK degree programme.

Erasmus: key facts

- You will be awarded a grant for a study or work placement (as part of your study programme) of anything between three to ten months duration.

- If you take up an Erasmus placement you do not pay tuition fees to the host university abroad.
- If the placement is for the full academic year then the tuition fee is also waived by the UK university.
- The Erasmus grant serves as a contribution towards living costs when abroad. In 2010–11 it was €225 per month. These grants are non-repayable and non-means tested and are in addition to any standard grant or SLC loan that you are entitled to (these may be adjusted to a special 'overseas rate'). Universities may, at their discretion, also offer Access to Learning funds (bursaries) to those who require additional money.
- Under the Erasmus scheme you need to gain credits for your studies in your placement university and have these transferred into your UK university programme.

Note that there is an inherent risk in undertaking an Erasmus placement in that the credits and the grades you study for in your placement university in Europe are instead of credits and grades you would have studied in your UK university – they are not in addition to these. Because grading systems may vary greatly across Europe you are open to the possibility of getting different grades than those you are used to receiving in your home university and this may affect your final degree classification result. For this reason you should check if the programme you will study will be in English, or if not, that you are strong in the language of delivery of the programme! It is best to check how your home university handles the credits and grades that the partner university sends them for your studies.

Useful website: www.britishcouncil.org/erasmus.htm

Applying to your universities

Time frame

Deadlines for application in many European countries are set centrally by the individual MoEs. Universities need to follow these deadlines and have little flexibility with them. It is important to check the deadlines and stick to them for your application because if you miss a deadline there is no guarantee that you will have a place in the university you want to go to. Deadlines can be quite early in the year.

Application deadlines

In order to know when to apply to universities in different EU countries the following website is useful: www.studyineurope.eu/application-deadlines

Application procedure

Many European countries operate a centralised application procedure for access to their universities. For example, Holland uses Studielink (info.studielink.nl/en/) and Denmark the KOT system (www.optagelse.dk/vejledninger/english/). Sweden has its pooled admission service (www.universityadmissions.se). In the UK, there is also a centralised application system run by a private company – UCAS – which undertakes this function in a similar way for UK universities. In this way the MoEs are able to keep track of how many places across the universities have been filled. Applicants need to make a list of choices in their application so that if the first choice is not available then the application goes to the second choice. You usually need to download the English version of the central application form from the relevant MoE website (most university websites will have guidance and links to this for you). To complete this form you usually need to find out and enter the code for the university and the programme(s) you wish to study and ensure the form is sent in by the stated deadlines for completion.

Apart from the centralised systems mentioned above, application procedures may vary somewhat from country to country, with more or less autonomy being given to universities over the process. In some countries the MoE needs to check the application that has been sent in to the universities and give final approval – and then the MoE themselves issue the letters of acceptance (this is the case, for example, in Romania). Others allow the universities to make the final decision and offer the letters of acceptance, but may have to rubber stamp the applicant's certificates. The MoE in many countries also controls the entry level qualifications that universities are required to use to ensure that international students have the equivalent level qualification from their own counties to be able to enter to study in the requisite national university system.

Note that ENIC (http://enic-naric.net) is an organisation that provides information on national education systems and makes recommendations for qualification equivalences. It is subscribed to by most MoEs and by many universities in Europe and is the basis upon which decisions about the kind of qualification is needed by European universities of their international students.

Also note that in many European countries, university programmes are designed centrally by the MoE. Universities then apply to run these programmes and are given a licence to do so and funding for this for a maximum number of student places. This means that the same programmes are on offer across many universities in the country. This is different from the situation in the UK where universities are responsible for designing and validating their own programmes and hence these programmes vary individually.

A Level certificates

If you are currently at secondary school taking your A Levels, you won't be notified of your results until mid-August, long after many deadlines for applications to universities in Europe. Many school leaving examination results in European countries are awarded earlier (May/June) and so you may find that the lateness of the publication of results in the UK is problematic, as in some countries universities may not be able to guarantee you a place until your results and certificates have been verified. As many programmes begin in September, this is problematic, especially if they are unwilling to accept the preliminary results slip issued in August instead of requiring official certificates from the examination board in question. There are several things you can do to try and overcome this problem.

1   Ask your school to issue a certificate (on headed paper) that is stamped and signed and confirms the A Level results you have been awarded by the examination board in question with the statement that 'these results are valid for application for entry to the UK university system'.
2   Contact the A Level board you will be taking your examinations with and request a speeded up sending of the final certificate to your home address. Most boards do have such a system.
3   Check with the university you are applying to that they will accept the preliminary results slip as evidence of your final A Level grades and that you will be able to enrol for the programme with this once you arrive there. Also explain that these results are used by UK universities for access to university programmes in the UK higher education system.
4   For some countries you may need to have your A Level and other certificates legalised by a Notary Public and then issued an Apostille Certificate by the Foreign Office. This will need to be done very quickly if this is the case. Make sure you know if either of these steps is indeed necessary.

Conditional offers

Because school leavers apply to universities before they have their school leaving examination results, UK universities have in place a system of conditional offers. This means that if you have applied correctly by the necessary deadline, the university will offer you a place conditional upon you achieving the necessary grades for entry in your school leaving examinations (in the UK these are A Levels).

The picture varies in Europe. Quite common in Eastern Europe is the system whereby all applications are to be sent in by certain dates. On these dates all the applications are assessed and the top ones allocated the places that are available. If, for example, there are 50 places available on a programme, then the top 50 applications will be offered places. Often there are two or more application rounds for the offering of places. One deadline for Round 1 may be at the beginning of the summer and Round 2 at the end, when any untaken places are filled. This system is very inconvenient for UK students as it means you cannot begin planning your study abroad until quite late in the year. Because of the lottery aspect to the system it also means that it is perhaps wise to apply to several universities to spread the chance of gaining a place. This increases costs, especially if these universities require legalised documents with Apostille Certificates and application fees!

Legalising your documents

There are two stages to legalising your qualifications:

1 Having copies of your certificates legalised by a UK Notary Public
2 Having these then given Apostille Certificates by the Foreign and Commonwealth Office.

You may only be required to do Stage 1 or you may need to do both stages. On the other hand, some universities may not require legalisation of documents or just require you to have copies of your certificates stamped and signed by your UK school or university.

University entrance examinations

Because it is in reality pretty much impossible to be able to efficiently and effectively select through comparing the best applications from the range of countries with all their various school leaving educational qualifications, universities may have devised an entrance examination system. This will either be their own entrance examination (which you will probably need to sit at the university itself on a specified date) or some standardised examination result such as a SAT subject test. This simplifies their task of selecting the 'top students'. Note that you will need to pay a non-refundable application fee and a university examination fee in these instances.

First come, first served

Another system, which is more akin to the UK model and more commonly found in Western Europe, is the first come, first served model. In this system a university publishes the minimum qualifications necessary to apply for a place from each educational system and then as students present themselves with these they are offered places. Note that in Holland and many Scandinavian countries, access to higher education is often dependent on simply having graduated from high school and so you may be surprised to be told not to worry about the grades you receive at A Level! Many universities state that to be admitted on to your chosen programme you simply need to have school leaving certificates that will let you enter university in your own country: this is often termed the 'general entry requirement'. What exactly this is for UK students can be a bit of a mystery if the university hasn't published lists of what these minimum entry requirements are. In order to be transparent some countries publish lists.

Any EU universities that can operate a conditional acceptance system will process your application when they receive it and give you an offer dependant on you achieving the necessary passes in your A Levels.

In this case, universities will probably want to see an indication of how well you are doing at school currently. This may be a request for your 'grades transcript for the previous three semesters'. The problem is that UK schools do not usually operate a semester system – with school exams at the end of each semester. In point of fact your A Level examination results will often serve as your transcript.

Preparation for the school leaving certificate in most European countries usually takes two years in most educational systems and therefore there are usually four semesters' (S1, S2, S3, S4) worth of grades awarded for studies for the school leaving certificate. The school leaving certificate is not the same thing as the school leaving examinations, which are usually national examinations like the A Level examinations taken on specific dates in the final year of study at school.

Because the UK system is based only on an examination system (A Levels) and not a grades system for a school leaving certificate, there is potential for misunderstanding over this and you may be requested to supply evidence of current progress which is in fact difficult for you to supply. You may have a termly grades sheet that you can use, but it is very useful to have prepared a reference from your school (similar to the one that is issued by your school for the UCAS application form that also indicates predicated grades). With regards to grades, it is also sensible to supply an explanation of what the grades mean in the UK school system. (There is a transcript form in the Appendix at the end of this guide that you may like to use as an example for this.)

The gap year benefit

If you take a year off (gap year) after school, many of the above mentioned problems are avoided as you will have all the necessary A Level certificates and results in time for your application. You will also have had time to visit the university and country before you set off to study and this will give you time to check out and sort out your accommodation. Indeed you will have a better chance of securing the first choice university you wish to study in as you will be ahead of most of the national applications from the country in question.

February start

Some university programmes may have start dates at the beginning of Semester 2, i.e. for the beginning of February. This may well be a useful start date for you to get all your documentation of certificates in order and give you time to sort out accommodation to your satisfaction before leaving.

Visa information

As a UK national and passport holder you do not require a visa to study in the EU or EEA.

Student life in the EU/EEA

Campus life

Many European universities are located in historic university cities. Typically the city has a student area – usually replete with bars offering happy hours and cheap student restaurants.

Many European universities are integrated more firmly within the cultural and social life of the cities they are a part of than is perhaps the case in the UK. This means that facilities such as sports centres are municipal with student and local people sharing them – with students having discounted entry upon production of their student cards. The same may be true of sports clubs and associations.

Many European cities host carnivals and festivals which are times when the local population indulge in local cultural activities and traditional events.

Accommodation and student living

Accommodation options are often offered and managed by universities, but not always. Some universities may not have enough university accommodation for all the students they enrol and there may not be as much help to hand as students in UK universities are perhaps offered. This may mean that once you have secured a place at university you will need to be quite proactive in finding accommodation in the private sector. You may also wish to do this if the university accommodation on offer is for shared rooms, or in hostels that are not up to the requisite standard – which can still be the case with certain Central and Eastern European universities.

Some students find that if they take out university accommodation for the first semester this gives them a good base from which to find private accommodation that is more to their taste. It allows them to discover the town they are in and get to know the area of the city that is most convenient and attractive for them to rent in and also to perhaps find flatmates among their fellow students they are likely to get on with. Most universities seem to be quite flexible with their accommodation contacts, allowing students to do this without penalty.

Healthcare

As an EU citizen, a UK student can obtain a European Health Insurance Card (EHIC). For information, go to www.nhs-e111-ehic.org.uk/. With this card you are entitled to free medical treatment. It is wise to check the exact cover provided in each country by the EHIC card and assess if any extra insurance is sensible to take out in the UK before travelling to the country.

Work while you study

As an EU citizen you are entitled to work in the EU as a student. The pay will vary according to the country, with higher rates of pay reflecting the economic strength and cost of living of the country in question. Generally, the chances of finding part-time work are enhanced if you know the local language, so this is a good motivation for learning it. Of course it is sensible not to work too many hours if the main purpose of being in Europe is to study.

Further practical information

The language barrier

One of the main concerns about going to study in an EU/EEA country is that of having to learn and use a foreign language. Of course, if you are fluent in one of the languages of the EU/EEA (other than English), this is an incentive for you to choose to study in a country where this is the national language. If you do not know the local language then this is an ideal opportunity to learn the language and get this extra value added to your CV. Learning the local language is a great opportunity and will bring rewards, not just in terms of your own future employability but for your own personal growth and development and for your social integration into your new location.

After you finish your degree

A recent study by the European Commission on Erasmus students (students who had spent time studying out of their country in another European country as part of their degree) found that Erasmus students were earning 20 per cent more in salaries than students who had not undertaken the experience. This tends to suggest that employers see the value of students who have undertaken study away from their home country and culture.

Chapter 10

Hong Kong

Orientation

Introduction

Hong Kong is a former British Colony (which remained under British administration for 150 years) which became a Special Administrative Region of the People's Republic of China (HKSAR) on 1 July 1997. The region is currently under a 'one country, two system policy' which means its constitution, basic law and existing legal frameworks will remain in place for the next 50 years. As a result, Hong Kong enjoys a large degree of autonomy.

Hong Kong is located on the southern coast of China and is comprised of Hong Kong Island, Kowloon Peninsula and the New Territories which include 262

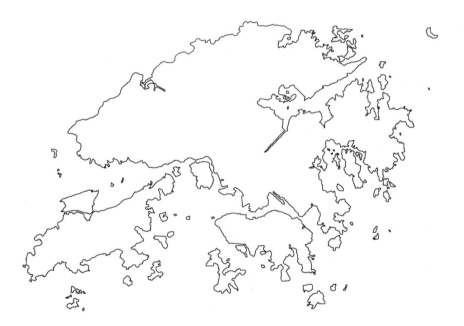

outlying islands. In Hong Kong, 95 per cent of the population is ethnically Chinese.

The official languages of Hong Kong are Chinese and English. The population of Hong Kong is around 7 million people, of which 97 per cent speak Cantonese (a spoken variant of Chinese that originates in Guangzhou). Mandarin is now also promoted and taught in schools in Hong Kong. English is also widely used by the legal, professional and business sectors.

Reasons to study in Hong Kong

- Hong Kong is an English speaking location which can act as a gateway for learning about, and understanding, modern China.
- Universities in Hong Kong are well-reputed and offer internationally recognised degrees.
- Hong Kong is ideally located in South-East Asia, and is within four hours of all major Asian cities by air.
- Hong Kong universities are compatible with the mainland Chinese higher education sector, meaning students can often choose to complete their studies in mainland China should they so choose.

Higher education in Hong Kong

Finding your course and institution

Hong Kong has eight government-funded universities, all of which use English as the medium of instruction for the majority of their courses (see Table 10.1).

Outside of these universities, the Hong Kong Academy for Performing Arts has also been given degree awarding powers, and will be of interest to students interested in the following fields: Dance, Drama, Film and Television, Theatre and Entertainment Arts.

Crash courses in Chinese are offered by many universities too, which can be an added benefit to studying at a Hong Kong university. Some programmes are run in Mandarin to cater for mainland Chinese students studying in Hong Kong.

Hong Kong has not focussed as much on international student recruitment as other neighbouring countries such as Malaysia or Singapore. Instead it has concentrated on making itself compatible with the mainland Chinese higher education market. Despite this, students will find that Hong Kong has world class universities which attract some of the highest calibre professors from around the world. In 2012, there were roughly 10,000 international students studying in Hong Kong (according to the UNESCO Institute for Statistics).

Undergraduate degrees in Hong Kong are usually four years in length, and the first year is usually general in nature (similar to US undergraduate degrees). Students then choose a major from the second year onwards. Taught Master's degrees in Hong Kong are usually two years in length. The academic term in

Table 10.1 Hong Kong universities using English as the medium of instruction

University	Key information
City University Hong Kong	Established in 1984. This was originally the Polytechnic of Hong Kong and assumed full university status in 1994. It has some 20,000 students.
Hong Kong Baptist University (HKBU)	Established in 1956. The university has a Christian heritage and offers programmes in Arts, Business, Chinese, Medicine, Communication, Continuing Education, Science, Social Sciences and Visual Arts. It has some 8,500 students.
Lingnan University	Established in 1967. Lingnan is the only Liberal Arts university in Hong Kong. It has 2,400 students.
The Chinese University (CUHK)	Established in 1963. The Chinese University is a leading research university offering upwards of 300 undergraduate and postgraduate programmes. It has some 20,000 students.
The Hong Kong Institute of Education (HKIEd)	Established in 1994. The university offers programmes in Education, Global and Environmental Studies, Language and Cultural Studies, Health and Education. It has some 8,000 students.
The Hong Kong Polytechnic University	Established in 1937. It offers academic programmes developing professionals for the business, industrial and social sectors. The university has an emphasis on workplace learning. There are 170 undergraduate and postgraduate programmes. It has some 28,000 students.
The Hong Kong University of Science and Technology (HKUST)	Established in 1991. The university is internationally recognised for its Engineering, Science, Business and Management programmes at both undergraduate and postgraduate levels. It has some 10,000 students.
The University of Hong Kong (HKU)	Established in 1911. This is consistently the highest ranked university not only in Hong Kong, but in Asia. It also has the largest international student population. It has some 18,000 students.

Hong Kong usually follows the UK model, with the academic year starting in September/October and finishing in May. The year is usually comprised of two semesters.

Due to the small number of universities in Hong Kong, students considering studying there should be able to spend time looking through each of the different universities in order to narrow down their choices. Students will find preliminary information about each university in Table 10.1 to start with, and may also find the 'Program Search' option at http://studyinhongkong.edu.hk/ useful.

Though decisions should not be made on university rankings alone, it may interest students to know that four universities in Hong Kong are included in the top 200 Times Higher Education World University Rankings 2012–13. These are: The University of Hong Kong (35th), Hong Kong University of Science and Technology (65th), Chinese University of Hong Kong (124th) and City University of Hong Kong (182nd).

The credit system

Hong Kong universities use the GPA system. This is on a 4-point scale (with some universities giving 4.5 for an A+ grade). See Table 10.2.

Financing your studies

Tuition fees and living costs

Tuition fees

These are set by individual institutions and for non-residents can vary between HK$75,000–120,000 (approximately £6,400–10,100).

Living costs

See Table 10.3 for more information on the general costs of living in Hong Kong.

Financial aid

Some Hong Kong universities offer international students merit-based scholarships. These are usually awarded automatically, and require no further application process (than that required to apply for a place at the university). These merit-based scholarships may be given out for academic achievement or for sporting achievement. For more information, students are encouraged to contact the university directly.

Student loans

There are no student loans available to non-local students.

Table 10.2 Grading system with GPA points

Grade	GPA	Grade	GPA	Grade	GPA
A+	4.30	A	4.00	A−	3.70
B+	3.30	B	3.00	B−	2.70
C+	2.30	C	2.00	C−	1.70
D+	1.30	D	1.00	F	0.00

Table 10.3 Cost of living in Hong Kong

Cost	Price
Application fees	Most universities charge an application fee, and this can vary between HK$300–750 (approximately £25–65).
Accommodation	Campus accommodation can vary between HK$5,000–20,000 (approximately £400–1,700) per semester. Private accommodation, however, can be much more expensive and harder to come by. Private accommodation can cost students between £400–750 per month.
Living costs	Everyday living costs in Hong Kong, including food and bills and social expenses, should come to between HK$30,000–50,000 (approximately £2,500–5,000) although this will depend on the student's lifestyle to a certain extent.
Health insurance	Many universities will offer students free medical treatment at their on-campus clinics, while for some services students must go to public clinics which will charge students. All international students are still advised to purchase health and travel insurance in the UK to cover them in Hong Kong before they leave.
Books and supplies	The cost of books and supplies should be calculated as being between HK$5,000–10,000 (approximately £425–850).
Transport	An Octopus Card should be purchased by students in Hong Kong, for a refundable HK$50. A total of roughly HK$8,000 (approximately £680) per year should be budgeted for transport costs.

Applying to your universities

Time frame

Many universities have early, main and late application deadlines (the early deadline usually being in November, the main one in December/January and the late one being in February/March.). Application fees will typically vary depending on which application deadline you hit.

Application procedure

Hong Kong has an integrated admissions system called JUPAS. However, to use this system you must have completed a Hong Kong Advanced Level Examination in the last two years, meaning international applicants must apply individually to the different universities. When looking at application procedures on university websites, students should follow instructions for what is often called 'Non-JUPAS Applicants' or the 'Non-JUPAS Route'.

International students will find that they are usually able to apply to Hong Kong universities online, without having to submit any documentation by post. Students will typically be required to fill in an application form and upload supporting documentation before sending off their application. Often students will find that they are not required to submit certified copies of any educational certificates during the application process, but are instead required to provide this upon acceptance to the university, bringing down application costs considerably.

Visa information

Student visas

International students need to obtain a student visa in order to be able to study in Hong Kong. This can only be done once students have been accepted by a university in Hong Kong. The university which has accepted you will then act as your sponsor and liaise with the Hong Kong Immigration Department over obtaining your student visa, which then needs to be fixed to your passport. Both the student and the sponsor need to submit various documents.

Documents that need to be submitted by the student

- Application for Entry to Study in Hong Kong (1D 995A)
- A recent passport photograph (attached to the above application form)
- A photocopy of their passport information page
- A letter of acceptance from a Hong Kong university
- A photocopy of proof of the applicant's financial support

These are the main documents that will need to be submitted, but students will be provided with guidance about the visa application process by their university once they have been accepted. Students should remember that the visa will need to be renewed annually, and that the process takes up to three weeks to complete.

Student life in Hong Kong

Campus life

Hong Kong prides itself on being a safe and vibrant city. It is a large cosmopolitan city with a mixture of Western and Chinese cultures, and students can expect the array of different social and leisure activities which are common of any of the big international cities of the world. Food is also an obsession in Hong Kong, and students will be able to benefit from a range of different food options from fast food (both Western and Chinese) to expensive restaurants. Popular fast food outlets in Hong Kong are the 'chan teng' (tea houses).

There are still cultural differences which students will need to be aware of before moving to Hong Kong. Chinese culture has its roots in Confucianism, and it is a good idea to understand the basic principles of this. Confucianism is a system of behaviours and ethics that stress the obligations that people have towards one another according to their role and position within society. There is a stress on duty, loyalty, honour, filial piety, sincerity and respect for age and seniority. The concept of face is very important, and involves showing due respect for another person's face (i.e. their reputation and/or sense of dignity). The Chinese also traditionally have three different names: their family name (which comes first), their first personal name (which is their father's personal name, and comes second) and their own personal name (which comes last). It is advisable for students not to use other people's personal names until invited to do so. Students may, however, find that Chinese students adopt Western names, which they may want international students to use with them.

Outside of the possibilities available in the city itself, students will find a variety of clubs and associations, sporting and otherwise, available to them on campus. Between their university and the city of Hong Kong, international students should be able to find an ample social life for themselves outside of their studies.

Accommodation and student living

If possible, students are advised to choose student residence accommodation in Hong Kong, as this can be considerably more economical. The drawback to this is that accommodation is often styled after American dormitories with shared rooms, which may not be an attractive option for UK students.

If students go for private accommodation they should expect to have to put a fair amount of time into finding it, as there is a shortage of accommodation in Hong Kong. As a result they should also expect to pay higher prices, varying between £400–750 per month.

Healthcare

Students will often find that they can get free medical treatment on campus, or will find that universities themselves charge students a healthcare fee for the use of such facilities. Some treatments, however, will not be covered, and students will be required to pay up from, or use the public clinics which charge HK$570 (approximately £50) per attendance.

International students are advised to take out private health and travel insurance before going to Hong Kong, and not to rely solely on the free medical care on campus which they may be able to receive.

Work while you study

Students are able to work part-time on campus for up to 20 hours per week, and are able to work full-time with no restrictions during vacation periods. If they wish to undertake an internship while studying, they may do so provided that the internship is related to the field of study and is endorsed by the university they are studying at. These internships may last for up to one academic year (or one-third of the duration of the programme, whichever is shortest).

Further practical information

Transport

There is a fantastic subway system and mass transit system that connects the major centres of population in Hong Kong. The airport is also very well connected, and students can benefit from a 24-hour bus service which crosses the city from end to end.

In order to travel between the main islands you are able to make use of a ferry service at a minimal price. Jetfoils also link Hong Kong, Macau, Shenzhen and other South China cities. To get to remoter islands there are ferry-like boats called 'kaido' or private hire boats called 'sampan'.

There are a variety of monthly passes made available by the Mass Transit Railway (MTR) for different routes. Once you know which route you will be travelling regularly you should consult the MTR website (www.mtr.com.hk/eng/fares_tickets/) to see which will be most relevant to you.

Students are also advised to make use of the Octopus card system for use on public transport, which works in the same way as the Oyster card in London. Travellers can use the card like a debit card on public transport and top it up at terminals. The cards can even be used in some supermarkets, vending machines and fast food outlets.

Mobile phones

There are five mobile network providers in Hong Kong: China Mobile Hong Kong Company Limited (PEOPLES), Hutchison Telephone Company Limited (3), SmarTone Mobile Communications Limited (SmarTone-Vodafone), CSL Limited and Hong Kong Telecommunications Limited (PCCW Mobile).

Weather

Hong Kong has a monsoon influenced subtropical climate. The temperature in winter usually hovers around 15°C to 20°C, while summers are mostly hot and humid.

Pollution

Air pollution is a serious problem in Hong Kong. The air quality is monitored on an Air Pollution Index (HKAICEMA). When levels are severe it is best not to do outdoor sports. Most of the pollutants are from nearby China, and while efforts to control the pollution are being put in place it remains a complex cross-border issue.

After you finish your degree

Students who have completed a higher education programme in Hong Kong may apply to stay under the Immigration Arrangements for Non-local Graduates. Those who apply within six months of graduation are considered 'fresh' graduates, while those who apply later are considered 'returning non-local graduates'. Those who apply as 'fresh' graduates are not required to have an offer of employment, while those who apply as 'returning' graduates are required to have an offer of employment. 'Fresh' graduates are able to apply before their results have been issued, but must have a 'proof of graduation' document from the university to do so. Once students have been granted permission to stay, they may switch jobs as many times as they like within the period the visa has been granted for without a problem, but will need to be in employment by the time the visa comes up for renewal.

Whether or not graduates opt to remain in Hong Kong after graduation, they should find that they have benefitted greatly from obtaining their degree in Hong Kong. Aside from the student experience, and the benefit of internationalising their CV, students will most likely have opened the doors to Asian job markets. Those who have taken advantage of their time in Hong Kong to learn Chinese will find that this is a major asset to their employability, and an understanding of Chinese culture will also be an attractive feature to any future employers.

Chapter 11

China

Orientation

Introduction

The People's Republic of China is the most populated country in the world, with roughly 1.3 billion inhabitants. It is the third largest country by land mass after Russia and Canada, and is divided into 22 provinces, four municipalities, five autonomous regions and two special administration regions (Hong Kong and Macau). Hong Kong is dealt with separately in Chapter 10 of this book.

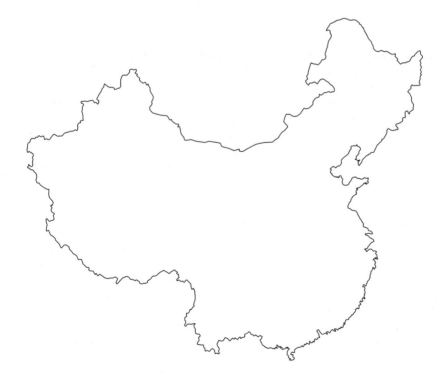

China is home to many of the biggest cities in the world, with Chinese cities regularly reaching a population of more than 5 million, and with several having more than 10 million inhabitants. The official language of China is Mandarin Chinese (Putonghua), although most Chinese people speak a regional dialect of this language. Cantonese is the main variant of Mandarin, and is spoken in the south of the country (Guangzhou, Hong Kong and Macau).

In the last ten years China has experienced some of the world's most dramatic economic growth at just under 10 per cent GDP growth per year. It is now the world's second largest economy after the USA. Chinese is subsequently becoming an increasingly important world language to know.

Reasons to study in China

- China is the fastest growing economy in the world and many international corporations do business in China.
- Learning Chinese will give graduates a distinct advantage in the international job market.
- Chinese higher education is recognised worldwide to be of a very high standard, with many Chinese universities ranking among the top worldwide.
- Experience a totally different culture first hand and take advantage of living in China to see many of the wonders of the world which are located there.

Higher education in China

International student education in China is nothing new. The country has hosted international students for over 2,000 years when students from East Asia and Arab states would traditionally come to study in China. Modern universities were developed in the nineteenth century, and today the higher education system in China has opened up to students from across the whole world. Today over 600 universities in China have international enrolments, and by the end of the first decade of the twenty-first century, the higher education sector was hosting almost a quarter of a million international students (either on language courses or full-length programmes).

Finding your course and institution

Most universities in China are public universities, although the private university sector is growing and now accounts for over 5 per cent of student enrolments each year. Public universities are tightly controlled by the Chinese Government and must maintain high standards, meaning that there are next to no accreditation issues with Chinese universities.

Students who are not fluent in Mandarin will need to look at the increasing number of programmes taught in English. While there are still more short courses in Chinese language, there are now universities offering full-length programmes in English. Students should note, however, that while the teaching will be in English, a basic level of Mandarin will be necessary to get by. For this reason, students intending on studying a degree in China are advised to do a language programme first. Students will find a variety of programmes in China are taught in English, ranging from Business to Engineering and Medicine. Students should use the 'Find a Program' feature on the CUCAS website (www.cucas.edu.cn/). (There is more about CUCAS in the 'Applying to your universities' section.)

Another good place to start is by looking at the programmes run through INTO. INTO is a UK education company that specialises in setting up joint ventures and programmes with universities both in the UK and abroad. As well as a variety of language programmes in different locations, INTO also works with Dongbei University of Finance and Economics in the city of Dalian, who offer undergraduate and postgraduate programmes in Business (taught in English). INTO helps students with a streamlined application process and on-campus support from their purpose-built INTO centre at the university. For more information you should consult the following website: www.intohigher.com/china.

Bachelor's degrees in China typically last four years, while Master's degrees can last either two or three years. Associate degrees are shorter, lasting two to three years. The academic year is typically divided into two semesters: one starting in September and running through to January/February, and the other starting in February/March and running through to July. Some international entrance dates are deferred to October rather than September. Students have one month holiday between January and February, and two months for summer vacation.

Students might be interested to find that the QS World University Rankings 2012–13 had the following Chinese universities in the top 200: Peking University (44th), Tsinghua University (48th), Shanghai Jiao Tong University (125th), Nanjing University (168th), Zhejiang University (170th) and the University of Science and Technology China (186th).

Financing your studies

Tuition fees and living costs

Tuition fees

At the time of publication, £1.00 (GBP) = CNY 9.46 (Chinese Yuan).

In general tuition fees in China are lower than in other countries offering programmes taught in English. The exact price of tuition will depend on which university you are applying to and the programme you are interested in studying.

Science degrees or specialised programmes like Medicine and Engineering may cost more, for example, than humanities degrees. As a general rule of thumb, tuition for most undergraduate and postgraduate programmes will be between £2,500–5,000 per year. Some programmes, however, such as MBAs can cost as much as £10,000 per year.

Living costs

See Table 11.1 for general costs of living in China.

Financial aid

There are no student loans available to UK students studying in China, however there are some scholarships available and awarded by universities for high performing students in the entrance exams. For more information on scholarship opportunities students should see the Chinese Scholarships Council (http://en. csc.edu.cn/).

Applying to your universities

Time frame

Applications may start any time from late February and responses are usually open until July (for September starts). Many universities will then require students to attend a university entrance examination (this will be in English for applicants to programmes taught in English). Universities will require between four and eight

Table 11.1 Cost of living in China

Cost	Price
Application fees	Most universities charge application fees, which can vary in price. As a general guide application fees are likely to range from £60–100 for each institution. The visa application fee is £180.
Accommodation	The price of accommodation will vary depending on where students are studying and whether they use university accommodation or private accommodation, but should cost no more than £2,000 per year.
Living costs	Living costs in China are very low, and students should budget around £2,000–3,000 per year on top of accommodation for utilities, food and social expenses. This means that total living costs should be estimated as being between £3,000–5,000.
Health insurance	The Comprehensive Insurance Plan of Foreign Students offered by the Chinese Ministry of Education (MoE) currently costs approximately £65 per year.

weeks to process applications and issue admissions letters and the accompanying JW210/JW202 visa form which students need for their visa application.

Application procedure

Students will typically need to attach certified copies of their A Level certificates and/or university transcripts (depending on whether they are applying for undergraduate or postgraduate programmes) to their applications. This means that students will usually need to take a year between completing their A Levels or previous degree before being able to start in China, as they will need to wait for those documents to be released. However, students can make use of this time to take a language course in Chinese to get up to the necessary basic standard before enrolling at university there. Students may also take this as an opportunity to experience China first hand before committing to pursuing a course in higher education in the country.

Trying to make sense of international application procedures can sometimes be a difficult task, as university websites are sometimes difficult to understand and English versions are often out of date when compared to the Chinese versions. For this reason, help might be needed in making applications to Chinese universities. One private company that provides such help in the form of a clear and concise website as well as an application service is the China University and College Admission System (CUCAS), which is similar to UCAS in its operation and can be found at the following website: www.cucas.edu.cn/.

They offer detailed information about studying in China and have a well-organised website that informs students about the different undergraduate and postgraduate programmes available for English speaking students. They currently work with 200 universities (although it should be noted that there are many more Chinese universities that do not work with CUCAS). They charge a fee for their service, which is in addition to the individual application fees from each university you apply to through them (up to a maximum of six).

Note: International students might be required to undertake a medical examination. This might be done before applying for a visa, or after arrival in China. The fee for this is typically in the region of £65.

Visa information

Student visas

Once students have received their acceptance letter and visa form from their university, they will need to apply to the Chinese Embassy for an X (Study) visa. The visa application fee is £180.

The X visa is only valid for 30 days from the date of arrival in China, during which time students must apply with their university for a Temporary Residence

Permit which will last the duration of their stay in China. The university will be able to help with details of how to apply for this.

Student life in China

Campus life

Students can expect life in China to be an altogether different experience from that which they might expect attending university in the UK. Adjusting to a different culture will take students some time, but can equally be a thoroughly rewarding experience. Students would be advised to seek out the numerous blogs that are available on the internet which talk about international students' experiences in China to get an idea of what to expect from their first few months in the country.

To a certain extent, the place where students are studying will greatly affect their student experience. Those in larger more international cities like Beijing or Shanghai are more likely to be able to seek out a more Western lifestyle than those in more provincial cities. Students will be able to find a variety of restaurants, cafés and bars in most Chinese cities to suit Western tastes, however, should they start to feel a little homesick. Indeed, international students will find China a very affordable place to eat out, meaning that they can take advantage of the country to lead an active social life. Most universities will also have a range of associations and clubs to join, similar to US or UK universities, providing students with an opportunity to meet and socialise with other students.

Students might be surprised to find that local food in China is not what they might have come to expect from Chinese food as it is served in the UK. Recipes and dishes in China vary from region to region, and what is commonly called 'Chinese food' in the UK is adapted from Cantonese cuisine. Food in the north of the country tends to be wheat-based, as compared to that in the south which tends to be rice-based.

Students should expect to receive a fair amount of attention from locals, particularly if they are tall, particularly pale or fair haired. This might be disconcerting for some students at first, but the attention will not be aggressive in nature, and students will get used to this over time.

China generally remains a very safe country for visitors and international residents. In fact, the most dangerous aspect of China is likely to be travelling on the roads, where officially over 50,000 people are killed every year. Students are therefore advised to be careful with regard to travelling by road.

Accommodation

Most universities will offer student accommodation, which is generally of a high standard. Indeed, many universities are building brand new state of the art accommodation for their students. University accommodation is often located very close to the campus, which can be important given the size of many Chinese cities. University dormitories usually include free wifi, laundry facilities, kitchen facilities and individual bathrooms for students.

Those who do not wish to live in university accommodation will need to register with the police within 24 hours of having moved into their private accommodation. Rental prices are variable across China from city to city, but students should expect to pay no more than £2,500 per year (for either university or private accommodation).

Healthcare

Students are required to purchase the Comprehensive Insurance Plan of Foreign Students offered by the Chinese MoE. The plan is contracted to Ping An Insurance Group and currently costs approximately £65 per year. Students will need to have health insurance cover in order to be able to register on to their programme at university.

Work while you study

International students are not permitted to work in China while they are studying at university.

Further practical information

Transport

China has one of the world's most developed railway systems, and students will be able to rely on public transport throughout the course of their stay in the country. Urban public transport in China is efficient, cheap and clean, if a little crowded, and journeys on the subway or buses should not cost more than between 10–50p.

Banking

Students should be advised that there may be a maximum amount students are able to withdraw from ATMs in China. For big payments such as rent or tuition fees, students may need to plan ahead or pay by bank transfer if possible.

Chapter 12

Singapore

Orientation

Introduction

Singapore is an island state at the southern tip of the Malay Peninsula. It is itself made up of 63 islands and is separated from Malaysia to the north by the Straights of Johor and from Indonesia to the south by the Straights of Singapore. It is a highly urbanised country.

The British obtained sovereignty over the island in 1824 and along with Malaysia it became independent from Britain in 1963. It then separated from Malaysia in 1965.

It is now the world's fourth leading financial centre and is also one of the busiest ports in the world. When considering the purchasing power index, Singapore has

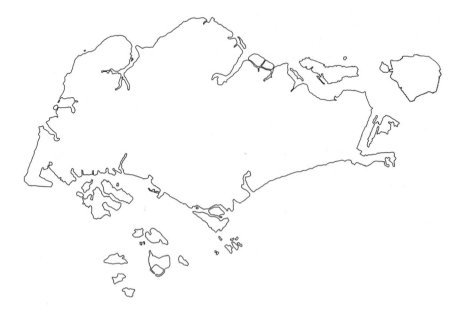

the third highest per capita income in the world. The population stands at slightly over 5 million people with the Chinese being the majority group (75 per cent) and with Malays and Indians forming the largest minority groups. Politically it is run as a 'unitary, multi-party republic', having had the same 'People's Action Party' in power since independence. It is a system that has delivered impressive economic development since its independence. It is a founding member of the Association of Southeast Asian Nations (ASEAN) and hosts the APEC secretariat (the Asia-Pacific Economic Cooperation), and it is also a member of the Commonwealth, the Non-Aligned Movement and the East Asia Summit.

Singapore has four official languages: English, Chinese, Malay and Tamil. The main religion is Buddhism (practiced by one-third of the population), with Christianity the next most professed religion followed by Islam, Taoism and Hinduism.

Singapore is an emerging educational hub and international student destination. It has the advantage of being a bilingual country in which two important world languages, Mandarin Chinese and English, are in regular use. Currently, however, it is concentrating on managing its education system so as not to disadvantage its own residents by offering too many places to foreign students. This means that foreign student numbers are capped, making it more difficult to secure a place as a foreign student than it used to be.

Reasons to study in Singapore

- You can study an international qualification from a Western University in an Asian location (Australian, UK, USA and European universities have campuses in Singapore).
- Singapore is a thriving business and education hub.
- It is an English speaking island and English is the medium of university instruction.
- It offers a modern infrastructure with universities offering state of the art facilities.
- It is a very cosmopolitan place to live and study.
- The application system is straight forward.
- The visa application and issuing system is simple and fast.

Higher education in Singapore

Singapore hosts some of the top universities in Asia. World academic rankings place the National University of Singapore (NUS) as the second in Asia after the University of Hong Kong, and the Times Higher Education World University Rankings place the NUS at 29 and the Nanyang Technological University (NTU) at 86. Singapore focusses on education, spending 20 per cent of its annual national budget on the provision of education. This focus has dual aims: to educate its own workforce to a high and competitive standard and capitalise upon this as a resource for the development of the country (Singapore lacks natural resources and therefore is competing globally in the 'knowledge economy'), and to attract international students as a source of revenue. In order to achieve these aims it has worked at developing itself as an international education hub. Much of this has been achieved not only by developing its own national universities but by partnering with prestigious international universities. The Government runs the 'Edusave' fund to help finance Singaporean students with their university education. These dual aims mean that there is a difference in fee levels between Singaporean students and non-resident international students at the universities.

Currently there are some 100,000 international students studying in Singapore and the aim is to increase this to 150,000 by 2015.

Finding your course and institution

A useful website to begin investigating universities in Singapore is: www. moe.gov.sg/education/post-secondary/.

In Singapore, there are currently five public universities (see Table 12.1) and two private national-supported universities (see Table 12.2).

Table 12.1 Public universities of Singapore

Public universities	Date founded	Size (No. of students)	Website address
National University of Singapore (NUS)	1905	33,000	www.nus.edu.sg
Nanyang Technological University (NTU)	1991	30,000	www.ntu.edu.sg
Singapore Institute of Technology (SIT)	2009	To reach 5,000	www.singaporetech.edu.sg
Singapore University of Technology and Design (SUTD)	2012	To reach 6,000	www.sutd.edu.sg
Yale-NUS College (YNC)	2013	To reach 1,000	www.yale-nus.edu.sg

Table 12.2 Private universities of Singapore

Private universities	Date founded	Size (No. of students)	Website address
SIM University (SIM)	2005	13,000	www.unisim.edu.sg
Singapore Management University (SMU)	2000	5,000	www.smu.edu.sg

Polytechnics: These consist of five local and six FSIs 'Foreign Specialised Institutions'. These are 'tie ups', i.e. institutions that work with foreign institutions to offer niche programmes. These polytechnics provide three-year diploma courses in a wide range of industry-related subjects.

As well as the national universities and the polytechnics, the higher education scene in Singapore also includes a number of private institutions of higher education as well as a growing number of foreign universities with branch campuses located in the country.

Note that as a way of trying to regulate the quality of the private universities offering courses in Singapore, the Government has brought in a quality certification scheme called 'Edutrust'.

Table 12.3 shows some of the international universities and institutes of higher education that offer programmes in Singapore.

Table 12.3 International universities and institutes in Singapore

Business and Finance	Websites
EDHEC–RISK Institute	www.edhec-risk.com/
INSEAD Asia Campus	http://campuses.insead.edu/asia/
ESSEC Business School	www.essec.edu/
S P Jain School of Global Management	www.spjain.org/
University of Chicago Booth School of Management	www.chicagobooth.edu/

Technology	
German Institute of Science and Technology	http://tum-asia.edu.sg/
DigiPen Institute of Technology Singapore	https://singapore.digipen.edu/

Other	
Tisch School of the Arts Asia	www.tischasia.nyu.edu.sg/page/home.html
Sorbonne-Assas International law School	www.sorbonne-university.com/very-definite-international-reach
Kaplan	www.kaplan.com.sg/
University of Nevada Las Vegas Singapore	www.unlv.edu.sg/
Lasalle College Of The Arts	www.lasalle.edu.sg/
James Cook University Singapore (JCU)	www.jcu.edu.sg/
University Of Nevada Las Vegas Singapore (UNLV)	unlv.edu.sg/
University Of New South Wales Asia (UNSW)	www.singapore.unsw.edu.au/
Curtin University Singapore	www.curtin.edu.sg/
The University Of Adelaide, Ngee Ann-Adelaide Education Centre (NAAEC)	www.naa.edu.sg/
Marketing Institute of Singapore	www.mis.edu.sg/

The credit system

The grading and credit system is designed to allow for flexibility as it combines features of the UK and USA systems. Credits are awarded for time spent studying and grades are either awarded using the USA GPA system (see Table 12.4) or using the UK final degree class awards system (see Table 12.5).

Table 12.4 USA GPA system

Grade	Grade point
A+	5.0
A	5.0
A−	4.5
B+	4.0
B	3.5
B−	3.0
C+	2.5
C	2.0
D+	1.5
D	1.0
F	0

Table 12.5 UK final degree class awards system

Grade	Scale	Grade description	US grade
I	70.00–100.00	First Class Honours	A
II	60.00–69.99	Second Class Honours, First Division	A−/B+
II	50.00–59.99	Second Class Honours, Second Division	B
III	40.00–49.99	Third Class Honours	C
	0.00–39.99		F

Financing your studies

Tuition fees and living costs

At the time of publication, £1.00 (GBP) = SGD 1.884 (also written S$).

Tuition fees

Singapore is not a cheap option for international study. Although tuition fees are not cheap they are still internationally competitive when compared to such countries as the USA. They can vary but as an indication, NTU charges around S$30,000 per annum for a Bachelor's degree (2013 entry). The private universities may charge a lot more. Note that there are reduced fees for Singapore citizens (50 per cent or more reduction) and a reduction (less, but significant) for Singapore residents. If you are applying as an independent applicant from the UK you are classified as a 'non-subsidised student' and are liable for the full international fee.

Living costs

Singapore also has high living costs by South-East Asia standards. All imported goods are expensive.

Financial aid

There are various schemes put in place by universities but generally for full-fee paying international students who wish to study in Singapore and then not be bound to working in Singapore afterwards, the options are minimal.

Policies are liable to change so the latest information should be checked on university websites. Currently all students (including international students) are able to apply for a Singapore Government Tuition Grant and if successful only pay subsidised fees. However, if in receipt of the grant, students – including Singapore nationals – are required to work in Singapore after graduation. This is currently for six years for Medicine, five years for Dentistry and three years for other degrees. This 'service bond' is in effect the contribution to repayment of the non-repayable grant.

Table 12.6 Living costs in Singapore

Cost	Price
Application fees	Depends on the university – usually minimal (e.g. S$30 or reduced to S$20 if paying online).
Accommodation	Campus accommodation is around S$200–450 per month. Hostel and private accommodation can vary (from S$350–1,000 per month).
Living costs	Food: S$300–500 per month. Public transport: S$50–100 per month. Utilities and Bills: S$50–100 per month. Books and supplies S$100 per month.
Health insurance	S$10 per month (university scheme).

Note: As an approximate guide, you should be able to live on about £500 per month

---

Grant information

If you have any questions on the tuition grant you can contact the following:

Tuition Grant Unit
Higher Education Division
Ministry of Education
1 North Buona Vista Drive
Singapore 138675
Email: MOE_tgonline@moe.gov.sg

Student loans

There is a system of student loans available. This is arranged through the universities. For example, at NTU this is organised with the commercial banks OCBC and DBS and covers only the reduced equivalent sum that a Singaporean citizen would pay. The guarantor can be of any nationality but needs to visit the bank in question when the tuition fee loan (TFL) application form is completed and have his/her ID certified (this can be done in an overseas branch). In Singapore, the application is then taken further in the bank in Singapore and once approved a disbursement of money is sent to the university to offset the tuition fees. The interest rate is commercial, with repayments beginning after a maximum of two years after graduation. Minimum repayment is S$100 per month and the repayment period is a maximum of 20 years.

Applying to your universities

Time frame

You should apply a minimum of eight weeks before the start of a programme and should really aim to apply for entry by February of the year in which you wish to enrol. The usual breakdown of semesters is into two 13-week long semesters per year from August to December and January to May followed by a special five-week term in the summer.

Application procedure

Most applications are made online to the universities with supporting documents being posted to the university. There is often a modest application fee to be paid.

Visa information

Student visas

All foreign students need to apply for a Student's Pass. To apply you must first be accepted by an HIL (Higher Institute of Learning) and then within two weeks of acceptance applicants need to make a visa application via the Immigration and Checkpoint Authority (ICA) (there is a small non-refundable application fee: currently S$90). The application should also be made at least one month before the beginning of the programme. Applications are made online by the submission of eForm 16 through SOLAR (the Student's Pass On-Line Application and Registration system). The processing time is usually a matter of days rather than weeks. Successful applicants are issued an IPA (In Principal Approval) Letter by the ICA and also an entry visa (no separate application is required for this). This allows entry to Singapore and once in Singapore you need to visit the ICA (you need to make an appointment) to undertake completion of formalities and be issued with a full Student Pass. There is another applicable small fee for this.

Note that you will need to have undertaken a medical report as prescribed on the ICA website.

The following website is useful for providing more details on this: www.ica. gov.sg/index.aspx.

Student life in Singapore

Campus life

Student life often centres on the hostels, which provide sports and recreational facilities. Many student clubs and a tradition of volunteering activities provide opportunities to get to meet local students and people.

Accommodation and student living

There are a number of student hostel companies which can provide a good place to start living and from which to later move out to your own private accommodation. These offer meal plans, security, laundry services, airport pick up and transportation services and can vary in the type of accommodation they offer from single en-suite rooms to shared rooms. The hostels are blocks of accommodation units usually offering other services such as a gym, library, sports fields and areas for socialising. As Singapore has a very good transport system the hostels tend to be located near to MRT stops.

A deluxe single room may cost around S$1,100 (£584) for three months which works out at less than £200 per month. A twin room is of course cheaper at around £170 per month.

A useful website to check out student hostel offers is: www.65hostel.com/.

Healthcare

Universities require students to take out their own organised health insurance scheme. This is compulsory for attendance at university but is minimal, e.g. S$120 for the year (which works out at S$10 per month). You may wish to take out private insurance as well to cover aspects not in any university scheme. Travel insurance, which it is wise to take out, also needs to be bought separately.

Students entering Singapore are screened for HIV and TB and applicants must prove they are free of these conditions in order to obtain a Student Pass.

Work while you study

A Student Pass in an HIL for an international student usually means that you are exempted from having to apply for a work permit. You can usually work for 16 hours per week during term time and up to 40 hours per week during vacation time.

Note: There are 26,000 international companies in Singapore.

Further practical information

Transport

The Mass Rapid Transit (MRT) system runs the length and width of Singapore. Traffic drives on the left and cities are entered by toll roads (electronic toll collection). The main islands are connected by ferryboat service.

Mobile phones

You can opt for either a pre-paid or post-paid mobile phone service. Post-paid means you pay for the service on a monthly basis and is best for those staying any length of time in the country.

There are three cell phone providers in Singapore: Singtel Mobile, M1 and Starhub. They vary slightly in the features offered and all offer competitive subscription plans. The three companies have reliable and country-wide coverage.

Weather

Singapore has a tropical rainforest climate. It is always hot and humid and it rains a lot! Daytime temperatures hover around 30°C and only drop to the mid-twenties at night. Most of the rains are between November and January (during the northeast monsoon). Sunny skies are not that common because of the cloudy conditions and the haze caused by pollution and smoke.

After you finish your degree

After graduating, international students in Singapore need to apply for an Employment Pass Eligibility Certificate (EPEC) issued by the Ministry of Manpower Singapore (MOM).

Successful EPEC applicants then need to apply for a one-year Visit Pass from the ICA to allow them to stay in Singapore for one year as they look for employment. Once candidates secure employment, the employer is required to submit an Employment Pass application to the Work Pass Division for consideration. Candidates are only able to start work after the Employment Pass application has been approved.

Chapter 13

The Caribbean

The Caribbean is the region that consists of the Caribbean Sea and its islands, of which there are more than 700. It has 30 territories comprised of sovereign states, overseas departments and dependencies. The total population is estimated to be just under 40 million.

What's available

The University of the West Indies (UWI) (www.uwi.edu/index.asp/) is a public university covering 18 English speaking countries and territories. It was originally set up as an independent external college of the University of London in 1948 and achieved independent university status in 1962. It now, however, follows the

USA university system of credits and GPAs. There are three physical campuses: Mona in Jamaica, Cave Hill in Barbados and St Augustine in Trinidad and Tobago. There are satellite campuses in Mount Hope, Trinidad and Tobago and Montego Bay, Jamaica, and there is also a Centre for Hotel and Tourism Management in Nassau, The Bahamas. To date it has had over 100,000 graduates.

UWI has seven faculties offering a wide range of undergraduate, Master's and Doctoral programmes in Engineering, Agriculture, Humanities and Education, Law, Medical and Veterinary Sciences, Pure and Applied Sciences and Social Sciences. While programmes are international in scope, they maintain a Caribbean focus which means that UWI is an interesting possibility for international students with an interest in learning about Caribbean society.

Fees and cost of living for studying at UWI vary according to programme. For example, studying Medicine for an MBBS at Mona Campus Jamaica costs £18,500 per year whereas a regular BSc costs some £10,000 per year. At the St Augustine campus in Trinidad and Tobago, tuition fees for UK students are charged at a US Dollar fee per credit. In a usual year it is usual to take 30–36 credits in which case a year's tuition fee for an undergraduate degree ranges from £7,000–10,000 depending on the subject area. Living costs are low, with accommodation (be it a single room in university halls or off-campus accommodation) costing somewhere between £1,250–2,000 per year. Estimated total living costs, however, are suggested to be about £7,000 per year.

> At the time of publication, £1.00 (GBP) = TTD 9.92 (Trinidad and Tobago Dollars); JMD 156.58 (Jamaican Dollars); BBD 3.092 (Barbados Dollars); BSD 1.548 (Bahamian Dollars).

Indeed, along with Central and Eastern Europe, the Caribbean has developed an international reputation as a region with a specialism in medical training.

> Useful website: A full list of medical universities is available at www.caribbeanmedicine.com/schools.htm/.

If you want to study Medicine in the Caribbean then it is useful to understand the difference between 'regional medical schools' and 'off-shore medical schools'. The former are geared towards students from the Caribbean who want to train and then work in the Caribbean, the latter are primarily designed as 'for-profit' institutions to train American, Canadian and other international students who after graduation wish to practice in the USA and Canada. These schools vary in their accreditations with top tier schools being ones accredited by all 50 US states. Such institutions are Ross MU (Dominica), AUC MU (Antigua and Barbuda),

St George's MU (Grenada) and Saba MU (Saba Island, near St Maarten). These medical schools prepare students for steps one and two of the USMLE (United States Medical Licensing Examination). Tuition fees per year (covering the two semesters) are in the range of £20,000–25,000. Room and board can be calculated at approximately £7,000 per year.

Pros and cons

+   It is a beautiful part of the world to study in with a wonderful all-year-round warm climate.
+   It offers state of the art medical universities that often have accreditation from US states.
−   Tuition fees for studying Medicine tend to be quite high compared to Europe.

Chapter 14

Dubai

Dubai is a city located within the United Arab Emirates. It is one of the seven emirates that make up the country of the United Arab Emirates. It has the largest population in the Emirates with just over 2 million people. Dubai is emerging as a cosmopolitan metropolis that has steadily grown to become one of the world's global cities. It is an important business and cultural hub for the Middle East.

What's on offer

A noteworthy world development in the supply of international education is the Dubai 'Knowledge Village' and its International Academic City area. This is

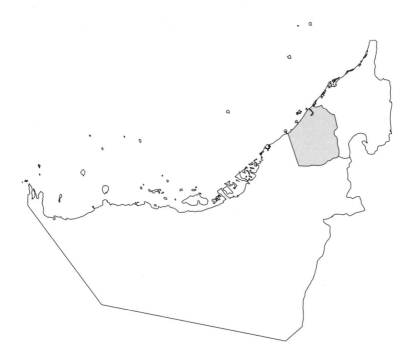

promoted as an educational 'Free Trade Zone', providing facilities for overseas universities to set up branch campuses. It is part of the UAE's drive to make itself a knowledge-based economy on a grand scale. Here there are a number of UK university campuses among the 13 international higher education institutes currently located in the DIAC (Dubai International Academic City). The aim is to have over 40,000 students studying in the DIAC by 2015. The development is still in its early stages.

Pros and cons

+   Dubai has an excellent international airport that is well connected to both the West (Europe), Africa and the Far East, which are all within reasonable flight duration times.
−   The cost of living in Dubai is fairly high (some £800 per month) and the tuition fees are relatively high (£8,000–12,000 per year) although this will vary according to each international institution.

At the time of publication, £1.00 (GBP) = AED 9.46 (United Arab Emirate Dirhams).

Chapter 15

India

India has a population of 1.241 billion and is set to outstrip China as the most populous nation on earth. The official language of the Republic of India is Standard Hindi, with English as the secondary official language. Note that individual mother tongues in India number several hundred and there are over 30 languages with over a million speakers.

Western education became ingrained in India during the establishment of the British Raj (1858–1947). The higher education system in India is now the third largest in the world after the USA and China. It is mainly run by the University Grants Commission, which enforces standards and liaises between the centre and the states.

India has 42 central universities, 275 state universities, 130 deemed universities, 90 private universities as well as five institutions established and functioning under the State Act, and 33 Institutes of National Importance. There are also some 33,000 colleges and 1,800 women's colleges.

What's available

Within India, the Indian Institute of Science, Bangalore (IISc) is ranked in first position with the Indian Institute of Technology (IIT), Bombay in second. The All India Institute of Medical Sciences (IIMS) is ranked third, The Indian Institute of Technology Kanpur fourth and the Indian Institute of Technology Delhi in fifth. The University of Delhi, the first fully fledged university, is sixth.

In the IIT the overseas fee is around £6,000 per year for an overseas student.

Note: You need to ensure the institution you want to go to is recognised by the Government. As India is growing fast, new establishments are being developed, but they may not be recognised. Indeed, driven by market opportunities and entrepreneurial zeal, many institutions take advantage of a currently rather lax regulatory environment and offer 'degrees' not approved by Indian authorities.

With regards to student visas, to be eligible for a student visa, applicants need to first be accepted on to a study programme. The visa covers the duration of the course, or five years of study abroad, whichever is less. The Indian Embassy in London has further information on the student visa forms needed. Their website is: http://india.embassyhomepage.com/index.htm.

Pros and cons

+   Although some institutions such as the IITs (Indian Institutes of Technology), IIMs (Indian Institutes of Management), NITs (National Institutes of Technology) and Jawaharlal Nehru University have been globally ranked and have global acclaim, they do not make the world top 100 and India still lacks internationally prestigious universities such as Cambridge or Harvard.
+   India is one of the world's fastest growing economies.
+   All university degrees are taught in English.
+   India is well known for its qualifications in Engineering and IT (mainly because of the IIT). The emphasis, therefore, at tertiary level is on Technology and Science.

+   India offers low living costs. It is estimated that £3,500 is enough to cover accommodation, food and transport in one year.
+   The Indian Council for Cultural Relations offers scholarships to students seeking to study in India. The majority go to students from developing nations but some are awarded to students from developed nations too. Other avenues for enquiry for scholarship are The Association of Commonwealth Universities (www.acu.ac.uk) and The Commonwealth Scholarship and Fellowship Plan (CSFP) (www.iccrindia.net/scholarshipschemes.html).
−   Keeping healthy is important in India. It is essential you have health insurance cover taken out before departing to study in India. Also ensure that you have had the necessary vaccinations (e.g. Hepatitis A and Typhoid) in good time and also have antimalarial prophylactics if you are in a risk area.
−   Students are not permitted to work while studying in India.

At the time of publication, £1.00 (GBP) = INR 94.72 (Indian Rupees).

Chapter 16

Japan

Japan is a country struggling with the problem of how to equip itself with a well-qualified global workforce that at the same time does not challenge long-established and cherished Japanese cultural traditions, language and identity. One way it is attempting this is to try and attract more foreign students to its universities – mainly

through scholarship programmes. In 2008, the Government announced the '300,000 Foreign Student Plan' (also known as the 'Global 30 Plan') which aims to take the number of foreign students from 140,000 to 300,000 by 2020. Currently the Japanese Government is aware that with only 3.3 per cent of its student population being comprised of international students (93 per cent of which are other Asian students), there is a need for change to make Japan a truly international destination. Japan now represents an interesting opportunity for UK students wishing to study, in effect practically for free, in some of the world's top universities.

The Embassy of Japan has the following useful website for those interested in checking out the study and scholarship possibilities: www.uk.emb-japan. go.jp/en/study/.

This website lists 13 universities offering undergraduate and postgraduate programmes in English. These are highly prestigious institutions and include the University of Tokyo (ranked 27 in the Times Higher Education World University Rankings), Kyoto University (ranked 54), Tohaku University (137) and Osaka University (147). Indeed, according to the QS World Rankings, Japan has ten universities in the world's top 200. Note that currently there are up to 30 universities in Japan where programmes are fully taught in English and this trend is on the increase.

Scholarship applications for the Japanese Government ('Monbukagakusho') MEXT scholarships are conducted through the Embassy of Japan in the UK (www.uk.emb-japan.go.jp). In order to study under this scholarship you normally need to undertake a year's preparation programme in the Japanese language at either the Osaka University centre for Japanese Language and Culture or the Tokyo University of Foreign Studies, before entering the four-year undergraduate programme at one of Japan's 87 national universities. After all, one of the main benefits of this study option would be to acquire a deep understanding of the Japanese language and culture (it is the third largest economy in the world) as well as to obtain a useful international qualification. You can, however, be accepted directly on to a university programme if a) your Japanese is at a satisfactory level already, or b) you wish to enter a programme that is taught in English.

Useful website for understanding the MEXT scholarships: www.mext.go.jp/ a_menu/koutou/ryugaku/boshu/1319122.htm.

The terms of the scholarship are that university tuition fees are waived and a stipend of £750 per month is made available for living costs and this covers the full five years of a regular degree (to include the preparation year if taken) or seven years if continuing on to a Medical programme. A return air fare is also included.

Note: Japan is a very expensive country to live in and you will need a minimum of £1,000 per month and more likely £1,200–1,400 per month to cover rent and other living costs.

Note: The Japanese academic year is from 1 April– 31 March.

Japanese university websites are clear and easy to use (see for example Kyoto's international website: www.s-ge.t.kyoto-u.ac.jp/int/en/). For the universities selected to offer international programmes, all the information is in good English and procedures for application enrolment, fees and payment are easy to follow.

Tuition fees are not high in Japan at around £3,500 per year for undergraduate studies. For example, the English language delivered Global Engineering programme in Kyoto University or the Automotive Engineering programme at Nagoya University are both £3,500.

The main problem facing the scheme is that Japanese corporate culture is quite closed and resistant to employing non-Japanese.

At the time of publication, £1.00 (GBP) = JPY 150.249 (Japanese Yen).

Chapter 17

Malaysia

Malaysia is an island nation in South-East Asia with a population of roughly 27 million. Malays make up 50 per cent of the population, with the other major ethnic groups being Chinese Malaysians and Indian Malaysians. The country is comprised of 13 states, with the capital being Kuala Lumpur.

Malaysia is increasingly trying to present itself as a serious choice for international students, and is working hard to internationalise its higher education market. Despite currently lagging behind neighbouring Singapore, the country has the stated aim of increasing its international student numbers to 200,000 by 2020.

What's available?

One strategy for developing international student study destinations in the country has been to open 'branch campuses' of foreign universities in Malaysia. Universities such as Nottingham University, University of Southampton, Newcastle University and Monash University have opened campuses in Malaysia where students can study for one of the years of their degree.

Many Malaysian private universities have also started offering twinning programmes, whereby part of the degree is studied in Malaysia, while another part is studied at a partner university in another country. These programmes are referred to as 2+1 programmes or 2+2 programmes. English is the medium of instruction

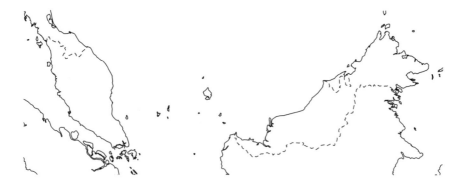

at most of the private higher education institutions in Malaysia, making it easy for UK students to study there. The same is true of postgraduate degrees in public universities, while most undergraduate degrees are taught in Bahasa Melayu.

Tuition fees at both undergraduate and postgraduate level tend to cost around £4,000 per year on average, while living expenses seldom reach above £4,000 themselves.

Some scholarships are available at postgraduate level for international students, awarding return air fares, the price of tuition and a maintenance grant of around £250 per month for living expenses. For more information please see the following website: www.studymalaysia.com.

Pros and cons

+   The yearly cost of studying in Malaysia is relatively low, as students can budget around £8,000 per year including tuition and living costs.
+   All universities (both public and private) are tightly regulated by the Malaysian Qualifications Agency (MQA) ensuring high standards.
+   The language of tuition is English across most universities.
+   Visa applications are easy and can be done upon arrival in the country provided you have a letter of acceptance from a Malay university.
−   Relatively small numbers of UK students choose to study in Malaysia (in 2008 only 13 UK citizens were enrolled on full-time higher education programmes in the country) meaning that those choosing to study in the country will be going into the relative unknown.
−   The international reputation of Malaysian universities is not yet at the same level as that of the universities in neighbouring countries such as Singapore and Hong Kong.

At the time of publication, £1.00 (GBP) = MYR 5.023 (Malaysian Ringgit).

Chapter 18

Russia

The Russian Federation has a population of 143 million and is the world's largest country, spanning 11 time zones. It has been one of the world's fastest growing economies and is now the eighth largest in the world. Over the coming years it has a predicted GDP growth rate of 3.4 per cent which reflects the fact it has an abundance of fossil fuels and precious metals.

Russia joined the Bologna process in 2010 and is now a member of the European Higher Education Area. It is reforming its higher education systems and is developing it to become more westernised. This process is in its initial stages and universities can consequently still be quite challenging places to study because of hangovers from the soviet period. The educational offer for international students is developing and Russia is switching its focus from a policy of recruiting students from the third world (a policy aiming at achieving political solidarity) to attracting international students from wealthier nations (a more capitalist aspiration). There are currently some 90,000 international students in Russia.

What's available

In Russia there are more than 600 state centres of higher education (which tend to focus on Science and Technology) and a large number (some 400) of private universities of varying quality which focus more on Economics, Business and Law. Higher education is delivered by universities (48) – these offer education in a range of subjects – and academies and institutes (of which there are 519) – which offer education only in specialised areas. It is interesting to note that there are no Russian universities in the top 100 ranking (Times Higher Education World University Rankings and QS World University Rankings). The top ranked university is Lomonosov Moscow State University at position 116 (QS).

Pros and cons

+ Generally the positive news is that tuition fees are relatively low, typically being between £2,500–5,000 and living costs are relatively low compared to the UK as well.

+ One fairly popular pull for international students are programmes in Medicine offered by the 50 medical universities in the territory. These programmes are taught in English for international students. General Medicine tuition fees are very reasonable as is the cost of accommodation (often this is shared accommodation). This makes it one of the most affordable places to study Medicine and attracts a good number of African and Asian students for whom it is affordable.

+ There are no standard entry examinations to be taken (such as the SATs in the USA) and each university sets its own entry criteria, which may include entrance examinations.

– The application process can be lengthy. Visa application documents (i.e. letters of invitation) are issued by the university applied to. It is recommended to count on at least three months for the application to be processed.

– Once a visa is issued it is for an initial three-month period only and needs to be registered within three days of arrival and then renewed in-country thereafter.

– A medical certificate attesting to a negative HIV status is required for students to be able to remain studying in the country (the test needs to be undertaken in Russia).

– It is essential to take out health and travel insurance before leaving the UK to study in Russia and it is also advisable to take an emergency health kit with you as some medical provisions can be hard to come by.

– Accommodation is difficult to find in Russia and so most students stay in campus university residences. These are also recommended as safer places to reside.

– Students need to be aware that there are problems of racism in Russia and non-white students need to be aware of this.

- English-medium taught programmes are currently restricted to a handful of universities (and are largely at postgraduate level), so most international students need to study in Russian. Students without the necessary level in the Russian language have to complete a pre-academic year and pass an entrance exam to be able to begin their studies.
- Further regulations are that students must be under 28 years of age for under-graduate and postgraduate studies and under 35 years of age for Doctoral level studies.

At the time of publication, £1.00 (GBP) = RUB 51.097 (Russian Roubles).

Chapter 19

South Korea

The South Koreans are also keen to attract international students to their country. To this end, many universities now also offer their programmes in English – especially at postgraduate level.

South Korea has three universities placed in the QS World University Rankings 2012 top 100: Seoul National University (37); Korea Advanced Institute of Science and Technology (63); Pohang University of Science and Technology (97). The Korean academic year begins late February/early March but most universities have two admission points in the year meaning you can begin your studies in September as well. Undergraduate programmes are four years with Medicine, Dentistry and Architecture usually taking from five to six years to complete. At postgraduate level there are two types of study on offer: generalist 'graduate' schools that offer programmes that focus on academic research and specialist graduate schools that focus on business programmes (MBAs).

Fees at undergraduate level are reasonable: for example, at Korea University, the tuition fee for an Engineering degree is in the region of £6,000 per year. Single-room campus accommodation works out at approximately £1,340 per four-month period. Off-campus accommodation can cost about £470 per month and other costs (bills, transport, food, etc. is estimated at £350 per month). There are many scholarship programmes available and it is quite usual for foreign students to end up with either a full or partial scholarship, i.e. covering 75 per cent or 50 per cent of the tuition fees. It is worth researching these opportunities on university websites. The following website of the National Institute for International Study is a useful starting point for this: http://studyinkorea.go.kr.

Note: The Government is actively making conditions propitious for international students to study in Korea by allowing students to take up part-time jobs and encouraging companies to take on international graduates after they have completed their studies (but companies do want international graduates to be able to communicate in Korean).

At the time of publication, £1.00 (GBP) = KRW 1,728.85 (South Korean Won).

Chapter 20

Taiwan

Taiwan is an island nation off the East Coast of China where the official language is Mandarin Chinese. The country is densely populated, with over 23 million inhabitants. Despite there being a large number of highly reputable universities in Taiwan, the country is less geared towards attracting international students than neighbouring Japan, China and Singapore. Despite this, the number of international students choosing to study in Taiwan is rapidly increasing. The country is trying to position itself as a gateway for Western students to study Chinese language and culture, particularly American students.

What's available?

There are an increasing number of programmes, both undergraduate and postgraduate, being taught in English in Taiwan, although the main language of instruction for most universities and programmes is Mandarin Chinese. Despite this, a wide variety of programmes can be studied in English, ranging from Chinese language programmes to Medicine and Engineering. The following website has a useful search function where students can search among the different programmes available by subject, language of tuition and location: www.studyin taiwan.org/.

Scholarships are available for students pursuing undergraduate and postgraduate programmes in Taiwan, and can award students between £500–600 worth of monthly stipend to help with living costs. Details can be found at the above website.

There are also a number of summer courses in Chinese available for students, which often involve travel and cultural activities.

Pros and cons

+ Students can study Chinese either alongside a degree or as their main subject (including summer courses), meaning that students studying in Taiwan can pick up one of the most important world languages of the twenty-first century.
+ Tuition fees are very low, with undergraduate degrees usually costing around £2,000 per year, and Master's degrees costing around £2,500 per year.

+   Living costs are reasonable in Taiwan, with a rough estimate of £450 per month to cover all costs (including private accommodation).
+   Taiwan is a country of astonishing natural beauty.
−   There are not a large number of international students in Taiwan, and most of those are from other Asian countries, meaning UK students studying in the country will be going into the relative unknown.

At the time of publication, £1.00 (GBP) = TWD 46.382 (Taiwanese Dollar).

Chapter 21

Turkey

Turkey occupies a unique position as it straddles Europe and Asia and is where the Christian world of Europe meets the Islamic world of the Middle East. It has a young population of some 74 million people and Istanbul has a population of over 13 million. Of the population, 99 per cent is registered as Islamic, although Turkey is officially a secular country with no official state religion – a result of Kemal Ataturk's reforms in the 1920s. Turks make up 80 per cent of the population and Kurds the majority of the remaining 20 per cent. Turkey has the world's 17th largest GDP. Its GDP growth rate was 9 per cent until a recent slowdown with only 2.2 per cent growth in 2012. Tourism makes up 26 per cent of Turkey's GDP.

There are 174 universities and academies (institutes of higher learning) in Turkey of which 103 are state universities. There are 66 private foundation universities. These were introduced into Turkey in 1974 and are the equivalents of private higher education institutes.

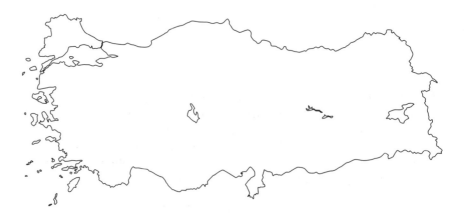

What's on offer

Turkey offers a number of English medium taught programmes in both public and private universities. Programmes can be found at both undergraduate (four year's duration) and postgraduate levels. Fees can vary considerably between the state and private sectors, with the former being from as little as US$500 per semester and the latter reaching some US$20,000 per year. Several universities offering English taught programmes are: Sabanci University (www.sabanciuniv. edu); Bosphorus University (www.boun.edu.tr); Koç University (www.ku.edu.tr); Yeditepe University (www.yeditepe.edu.tr); Fatih University (www.fatih.edu.tr) and Birkent University (www.bilkent.edu.tr).

A useful website for further information about studying in Turkey is: http://studyinturkey.com/.

Pros and cons

+ Turkey offers a low living expenses environment with accommodation, food and books costing between US$3,500–4,000 per semester (£4,700–5,400 per year).
+ Turkey offers a cosmopolitan environment and acts as a bridge to Westerners wanting to discover and understand the Islamic world.
+ Foundation universities offer a range of merit scholarships to students.
− The Turkish Government is keen to increase the number of international students in Turkey and there are scholarship schemes in place but these are targeted at Turkish nationals or students from other Turkic countries.

At the time of publication, £1.00 (GBP) = TRY 2.976 (Turkish Lira).

Chapter 22

Ukraine

Ukraine is one of the most populated countries in Europe, with around 45 million inhabitants. The country is not currently part of the EU, but may apply for EU membership in the near future. Ukraine currently hosts almost 40,000 international students, although most of these come from neighbouring countries like Russia.

What's available?

International students tend to be interested in Dentistry and Medicine programmes which are available in Ukraine taught in English. These courses are often considerably cheaper than they would be in EU countries, costing between £2,000–3,000 per year in tuition. Living costs are also considerably cheaper in

Ukraine with accommodation and health insurance costing students around £2,000 per year.

Other English language programmes are available in the fields of Engineering and Business Studies with similarly low tuition fees.

Pros and cons

+ Tuition and living costs in Ukraine are very low, meaning that studying in Ukraine can be an affordable option for UK students.
− Whereas students studying Medicine and Dentistry in the EU are eligible to apply to register with the GMC (General Medical Council) and the GDC (General Dental Council) in the UK without any further examinations, this is not the case for graduates of Ukrainian universities.
− Similar to Russia, Ukraine still suffers from problems of racism and xenophobia, which is something students should bear in mind when applying.

At the time of publication, £1.00 (GBP) = UAH 12.556 (Ukrainian Hryvnia).

Appendix

Transcript form for use in applying to your universities

School headed paper with school name and crest

School contact details:

TRANSCRIPT

Student name:

Description of school e.g. The Hodgkin's Technology School is a partially selective, mixed ability comprehensive school, with designated technology status situated in Buckwash, Bucktonshire. It encompasses Years 7 to 11 (offering GCSEs) as well as a sixth form college encompassing Years 12 and 13 (offering AS and A Levels).

UK Year 11 (Age 16) (Dates: e.g. 2006–7)
GCSE Results (State Exams taken in UK Year 11)
Pass Grade Range: A*, A, B, C, D, E, F, G (Fail = U)

Subject	Date (month/year)	Grade awarded
e.g. English Language	06/10	A*
etc.		

UK Year 12 (Age 17) (Dates: e.g. 2007–8)
AS Level Results (State Exams taken in UK Year 12)
Pass Grade Range: A*, A, B, C, D, E (Fail = U)

Subject	Date (month/year)	Grade awarded
e.g. Spanish	06/11	A
etc.		

UK Year 13 (Terminal year at high school in UK, Age 18) (Dates: e.g. 2008–9)
A Level Results
Pass Grade Range: A*, A, B, C, D, E (Fail = U)

Subject	Date (month/year)	Grade awarded
e.g. History	06/12	B
etc.		

Index

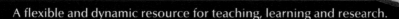